THINKING TOOLS FOR KIDS

An Activity Book for Classroom Learning

ASQ FOX VALLEY
Section 1208

ALSO AVAILABLE FROM ASQ QUALITY PRESS

Tools and Techniques to Inspire Classroom Learning
Barbara A. Cleary, Ph.D. and Sally J. Duncan

Orchestrating Learning with Quality
David P. Langford and Barbara A. Cleary, Ph.D.

Kidgets: And Other Insightful Stories About Quality in Education
Maury Cotter and Daniel Seymour

Total Quality for Schools: A Suggestion for American Education
Joseph C. Fields

Total Quality for Schools: A Guide for Implementation
Joseph C. Fields

Futuring Tools for Strategic Quality Planning in Education
William F. Alexander and Richard W. Serfass

Improving Student Learning: Applying Deming's Quality Principles in Classrooms
Lee Jenkins

The New Philosophy for K-12 Education: A Deming Framework for Transforming America's Schools
James F. Leonard

THINKING TOOLS FOR KIDS

An Activity Book for Classroom Learning

Barbara A. Cleary
Sally J. Duncan
Illustrations by Linda P. Kretzler

ASQ Quality Press
Milwaukee, Wisconsin

American Society for Quality, Quality Press, Milwaukee, WI 53203
© 2008 by ASQ
All rights reserved. Published 2008.
Printed in the United States of America.

14 13 12 11 10 09 08   5 4 3 2 1

Library of Congress Cataloging-in-Publication Data

Cleary, Barbara A., 1940-
Thinking tools for kids : an activity book for classroom learning / Barbara A. Cleary, Sally J. Duncan; illustrations by Linda P. Kretzler. — Rev. ed.
   p. cm.
Includes index.
ISBN 978-0-87389-737-2
1. Thought and thinking—Study and teaching (Elementary)—United States. 2. Education, Elementary—Activity programs—United States. I. Duncan, Sally J., 1942- II. Title.

LB1590.3.C55 2008
72.13--dc22

2008002932

No part of this book may be reproduced in any form or by any means, electronic, mechanical, photocopying, recording, or otherwise, without the prior written permission of the publisher.

Publisher: William A. Tony
Acquisitions Editor: Matt T. Meinholz
Project Editor: Paul O'Mara
Production Administrator: Randall Benson

ASQ Mission: The American Society for Quality advances individual, organizational, and community excellence worldwide through learning, quality improvement, and knowledge exchange.

Attention Bookstores, Wholesalers, Schools, and Corporations: ASQ Quality Press books, videotapes, audiotapes, and software are available at quantity discounts with bulk purchases for business, educational, or instructional use. For information, please contact ASQ Quality Press at 800-248-1946, or write to ASQ Quality Press, P.O. Box 3005, Milwaukee, WI 53201-3005.

To place orders or to request a free copy of the ASQ Quality Press Publications Catalog, including ASQ membership information, call 800-248-1946. Visit our Web site at www.asq.org or http://www.asq.org/quality-press.

∞ Printed on acid-free paper

Quality Press
600 N. Plankinton Avenue
Milwaukee, Wisconsin 53203
Call toll free 800-248-1946
Fax 414-272-1734
www.asq.org
http://www.asq.org/quality-press
http://standardsgroup.asq.org
E-mail: authors@asq.org

TABLE OF CONTENTS

A Letter to Parents and Teachers   viii

How to Use This Book   ix

Special Note for Teachers   xi

A Note to Students   xiv

SECTION I: TOOLS FOR COLLECTING IDEAS — 2

1. Brainstorming   2
2. Affinity Exercises   20
3. Lotus Flower Diagrams   34

SECTION II: TOOLS FOR MAKING CONNECTIONS — 48

4. Fishbone Diagrams   48
5. Relations Diagrams   62

SECTION III: TOOLS FOR RECORDING DATA — 78

6. Check Sheets   78
7. Flowcharts   90

SECTION IV: TOOLS FOR SEEING PATTERNS — 108

8. Histograms: Bar Charts   108
9. Line Graphs   126
10. Pareto Diagrams   142
11. Putting It All Together   157

Suggestions for Further Reading   173

Glossary   175

Index   179

LIST OF ILLUSTRATIONS

I.1　PDSA cycle
I.2　Matrix for suggested use of tools

1.1　Card for ranking items
1.2　List with rankings
1.3　Crawford slip for science project

2.1　Fourth of July brainstorming
2.2　Fourth of July affinity exercise
2.3　Affinity chart
　　　Affinity Diagram Template

3.1　Blank lotus flower diagram
3.2　What Nana likes
3.3　Golf and bicycling ideas
3.4　Gifts under $15
　　　Lotus Flower Diagram Template

4.1　Causes for successful play
4.2　French toast fishbone diagram
4.3　Too much milk: Fishbone diagram
　　　Fishbone Diagram Template

5.1　Paul's family
5.2　Lee family
5.3　Issues related to playground use
5.4　Issues and their relationships
　　　Relations Diagram Template

6.1　Homework completed
6.2　Carlos's collection sheet (partial list of customers)
6.3　Backpack items
6.4　Weather check sheet
　　　Check Sheet Template

7.1　Symbols for flowcharts
7.2　Anya's process flowchart
7.3　Decision point
7.4　Anya's check sheet
7.5　Crossword puzzle
7.6　Crossword puzzle flowchart
7.7　French toast flowchart
　　　Flowchart Template

8.1　Amounts in everyone's collections: Check sheet
8.2　Amounts in everyone's collections: Histogram
8.3　Visits to the nurse's office: Histogram
8.4　Gathering data for histogram with check sheet
8.5　Tallying numbers for histogram of heights
8.6　Normal distribution on histogram
　　　Histograms Template

9.1　Erin's empty line graph
9.2　Mr. Badgekar's departure times
9.3　Erin's piano practice record
9.4　Ariyah's pennies: Line graph
　　　Line Graph Template

10.1　Bird sightings: Check sheet
10.2　Bird sightings: Pareto diagram
10.3　Birds seen in Vermont: Pareto diagram
10.4　Colors of small chocolate candies: Pareto diagram
10.5　Colors of crayons in box
10.6　Multiplication facts: Pareto diagram
　　　Pareto Diagram Template

11.1　Check sheet: My homework data
11.2　Student information form for parents/guardians
11.3　Class bar graph
11.4　Class line graph
11.5　"Mad Minute" math facts assessment results
11.6　Math line graph
11.7　Math bar graph

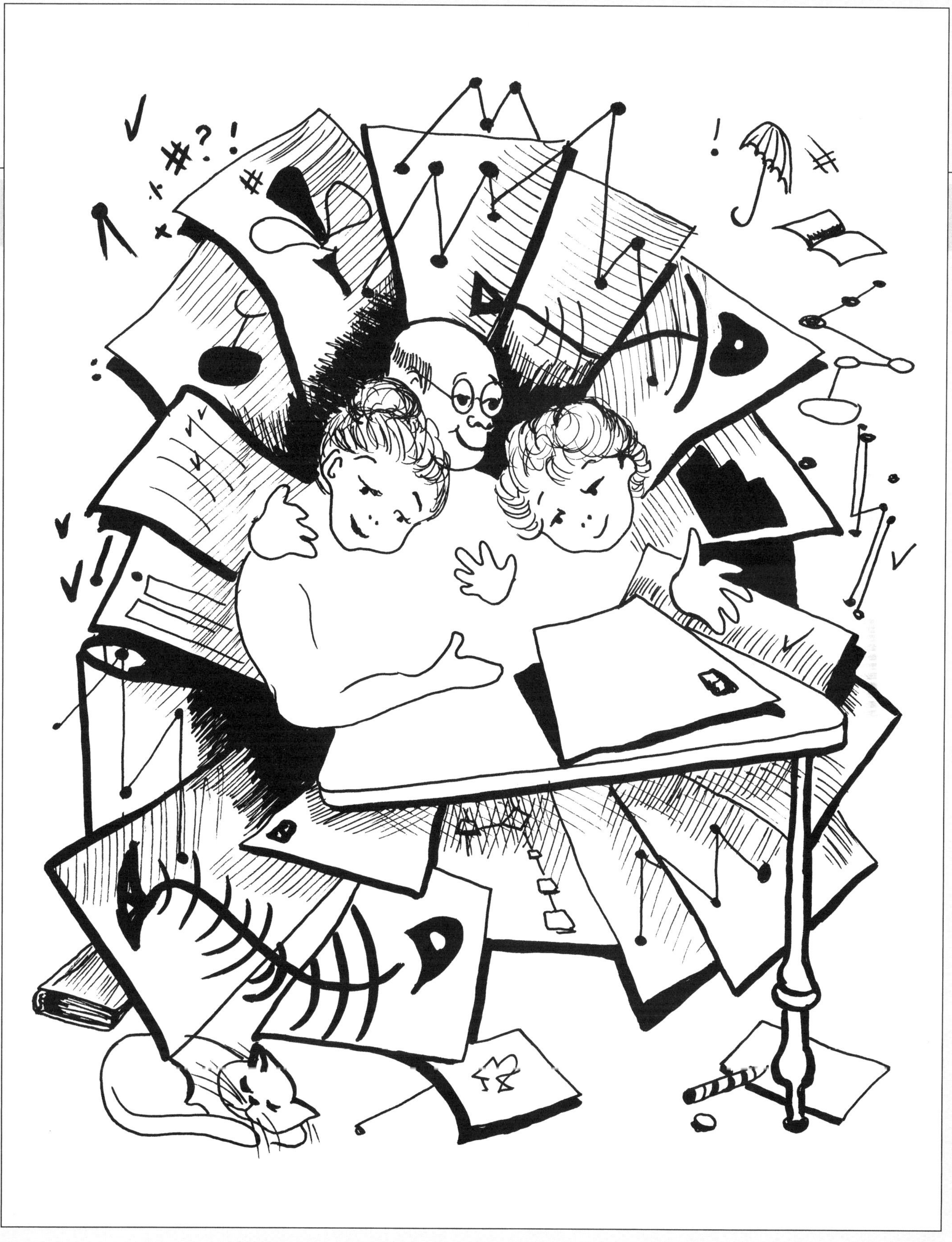

A LETTER TO PARENTS AND TEACHERS

What children are able to learn and know in the twenty-first century is dramatically different from what they would have learned and known if they had been born in the first or fifth century. It is certainly different from their learning in prehistoric days.

For those who lived in those earlier times, it was possible to have at one's disposal virtually all of the knowledge that was available to humankind, and to become familiar with it during one's lifetime. The body of knowledge that a caveman required was limited indeed, with respect to skills, understandings, and attitudes. A prehistoric human being could literally know everything in his or her world. A monk in the Middle Ages might have access to the body of knowledge that represented all known thought. With limited print materials, a well-educated person could read all the books in the world—literally.

Increasingly, information has become more complex as well as more prolific. In our lifetime, it is clearly impossible to know everything in our world, or even in a small aspect of that world. Furthermore we can no longer expect children to simply acquire the skills and knowledge that they need to deal with life, since we have little idea what their lives will be by the time they reach adulthood. And yet we must provide an education for this uncertain life.

Since the beginning of our public school system, the emphasis of education has been primarily one of acquiring information. With accessible technologies putting virtually everything at one's fingertips, the question now is how to connect different kinds of information so that it will have meaning, and how to determine which information is indeed useful.

What we can expect to give children includes the tools they will need to sort through information and make it meaningful. They will need to connect what they learn to what they already know and to apply it to new and complex situations. They will need to evaluate and assess what they know and how to improve on their own learning. Their lives will require a variety of problem-solving skills—not just logical, but aesthetic, interpersonal, kinesthetic, and other problem-solving skills as well. Skills of problem solving, process, and analysis will be more critical to their learning than any single body of information that they may access in school.

This book is designed to give young people tools to gather data, create information from that data, and reflect on the meanings that accrue from the process of gathering and analyzing data. These are improvement tools. They are also thinking tools.

For students to grow and learn, they must be able to plan their own learning, take steps to improve it, evaluate the outcomes, and make changes that are appropriate to improvement. This process, known to some as the plan-do-study-act cycle made popular by organizational theorist W. Edwards Deming, is a variation of the scientific method. Rather than jumping to conclusions, students in a complex world must build their own knowledge by pursuing this cycle over and over again.

The tools that are introduced in this book seem to be presented as isolated exercises. Certainly they are represented separately, with steps to learn each tool in turn. To be most effective, however, they should be applied to a larger process once they have been learned. While it is not within the purview of this book to describe or instruct in the scientific method or the plan-do-study-act cycle, there are sources for such instruction. These may be found in the education community as well as the world of process study and organizational change.

The purpose of this activity book is not to introduce tools for improvement as ends in themselves. The purpose is to help young people take charge of their own learning by applying some of these tools to their cognitive and analytical processes, both in school and outside, and to have fun while they're doing this.

HOW TO USE THIS BOOK

You will see many references to teamwork in solving problems or generating ideas. Learning of individual students is often enhanced by working with others toward a common purpose. Of course, one of the most important teams is made up of teachers and parents who work together for the enhancement of a child's learning. Home and classroom offer mutual opportunities for reinforcement of skills, knowledge, and attitudes, and for connecting learning into a continuous whole, rather than isolated, fragmented segments.

You will find the tools themselves grouped with other tools that may be used for similar purposes. Each tool is flexible, however, and this grouping is not meant to suggest that it can be used for no other purpose.

To get the most out of what this book offers, we suggest that teachers and parents continually place the tools within the learning context of the classroom or home. They can help young people to use several tools together to solve a complex problem or evaluate possible alternatives, for example.

The preface for students promises that this book is meant to help them do their best work. As a parent you can support that end by doing the following:

- Providing a model of learning for them, in which it is all right to reflect on failings and to gain from them

- Coaching them to examine their own learning, looking back on past performances and taking pride in present learning
- Instructing them in ways to improve their learning, including the use of these and other tools for improvement
- Providing contexts within which learning takes place
- Making it fun to learn; if these tools do not support that end for you, use others

The tools in this book can be used at home and at school. In each chapter, young people are summoned to try them out. Two sections, "Now it's your turn..." and "Home connection," give suggestions about tasks that can be pursued to reinforce the chapter's learning. When students make them their own, through practice and reflection, they are ready to learn more sophisticated tools that will be appropriate to improvement and continuous learning. This book represents only a small handful of the many strategies that are available to support learning.

To get the most out of this book, take time to go over the student's work with him or her, and talk about the learning. Help the student to use and apply the tools, both in the activity pages of this book and in real-life situations.

Use the tools yourself when they seem appropriate. Practice them with your child whenever you can.

Help your child, both in the classroom and at home, to see that learning is enjoyable, and that using different tools to improve learning offers an opportunity for creativity and fun. The tools will help students to become better prepared to take charge of their own learning as they go through life.

We have designed the chapters to be fun, but our emphatic purpose is to draw students into understanding some ways in which they can go about addressing both simple and complex issues that face them, not only in the classroom, but as members of families, neighborhoods, and groups with common aims.

Please discuss these tools with your child's teacher. Share ideas or applications that have worked for you. Like any tool, this collection can be used in a thousand creative ways. In the hands of young people, their applications are nearly limitless.

We hope that working with your own child to develop these thinking and learning skills will be not only productive, but fun for both of you.

SPECIAL NOTE FOR TEACHERS

Although parents will most certainly be involved in its use, this guide is designed primarily for classroom use by students. Our emphatic purpose, as we have said above, is to draw young people into understanding some ways in which they can go about addressing both simple and complex issues that face them, not only in the classroom, but as members of families, neighborhoods, and groups with common aims.

This book is designed for young people, to give them practice in developing habits of mind and skills to learn. The book does not provide instruction for adults about the tools. A number of instructive materials are available for adults—teachers and administrators who want more complete description of the tools represented here, as well as discussion of how and when to use each tool within the context of genuine student improvement. We would love, for example, to repeat our own descriptions of tools offered in *Tools and Techniques to Inspire Classroom Learning*. However, that would be not only redundant but outside the purview of this book as well.

We see this guide as a logical next step for classrooms whose teachers have already begun to be interested in how the improvement process relates to learning itself. In a way, it is a sequel to our earlier collection, *Tools and Techniques to Inspire Classroom Learning*, which is designed for adult facilitators rather than student learners. This book also supports a variety of other contexts in which the learning process is presented, from that of ASQ's Koalaty Kid Initiative to those created within school districts across the country.

In their planning process, teachers may articulate to students (and their parents) what young people will be able to know and do when they complete a term or a unit or a year of school. When they plan student learning in this way, they can then take the appropriate steps to make sure that their students move toward knowing and doing in meaningful ways. These tools are meant to support this process.

In fact, these tools are meant *only* to support the learning improvement process. Without this context, they are only stories of other people's children and the ways they go about improving their learning or their lives. There will be no child in any classroom or family who is exactly like any of the young people in this book—Erin, or Ariyah, or Charlie, or Madison, or Jake. The stories are meant to help other students connect their own experiences to those of the children in the book, and to reflect on the ways that they can improve.

Other resources can suggest ways to understand the learning process itself, in order to make the connections between that process and what is to be done in the classroom.

We suggest that you ask your students' parents to read this introduction to the book. Either send the book home with the child, or copy the letter and send it home. Your partnership with parents is critical to the success of your students as they pursue the learning process.

At the end of the introductory pages for students, you will find a chart with suggested uses for the tools (see Figure I.2). This is not meant to say that a tool has only one use. Think of the times you've used a staple remover to dislodge a thumbtack, or a screwdriver to pry something open. These thinking tools are meant to be flexible and to invite creativity.

In every chapter, you will find a section entitled "My Own Thinking Tools Page." These pages are perforated, so your students will be able to tear them out and make their own booklets. If you do not have enough copies of the books, you may want to make copies of these pages and give them to your students. It is important to encourage students to create thinking tools pages that reflect their own applications of the tools.

At the conclusion of this book, we have provided a short list of references that we believe will be useful both for instruction about specific tools and for understanding learning.

A glossary is also included, with definitions of various terms that have been used in this guide. However, because one does not usually learn meanings from definitions alone, the following is offered as a brief discussion of the larger purposes of utilizing these tools.

I. Support the Learning Process

Each of the tools described in this guide contributes to the learning experience in a unique way. Because they are *tools,* rather than content or information, they are designed to do the following:

- Help students take responsibility for their learning
- Allow for self-correction
- Build an understanding of the process of basing conclusions on data
- Promote interaction in the learning process
- Create an atmosphere of involvement
- Support reflection on the learning process itself

II. Provide Specific Strategies for Improvement of Processes in the Classroom

Together, the tools are often used at various stages of an improvement cycle, which reflects the plan-do-study-act cycle, otherwise known as the Deming cycle, a variation of the scientific method (Figure I.1).

```
        ACT  | PLAN
       ------+------
       STUDY | DO
       
       DEMING CYCLE
```

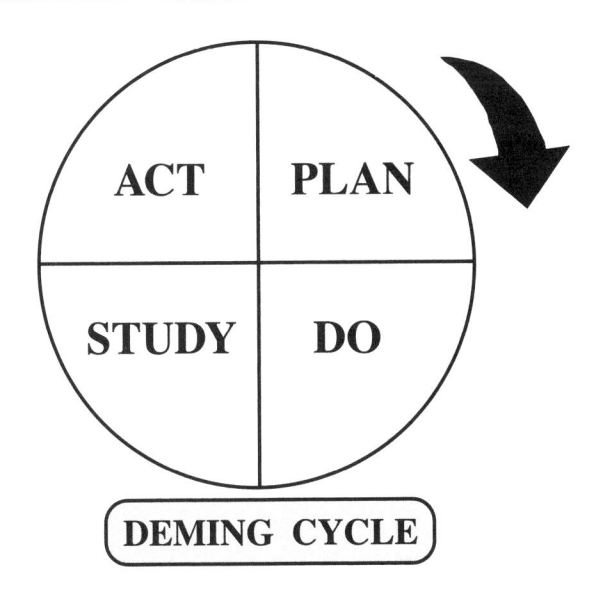

FIGURE I.1 PDSA cycle

A seven-step articulation of this cycle is reflected in the *Total Quality Transformation* model (Ball et al. 1990, 1994).

Plan:

Define the current situation or system: Understand the processes or systems that will be improved (example: process for learning spelling); gather baseline data for definition of the system.

Assess the current situation: Gather data to describe the processes as they are currently working.

Analyze causes: Identify causes of variation or problems and develop theories to address these.

Do:

Try out a theory of how to improve the current situation or system: Test ideas on a small scale.

Study:

Study the results: Determine the impact of the test actions by using data.

Act:

Standardize the actions: If the theory has been successful, apply it more widely throughout the system.

Plan for ongoing improvement: Continue to gather data and monitor the process for continuous improvement or select another process to address.

It would be a mistake, however, to view the tools presented here as components only of a specific continuous improvement process, or to feel that none of them is to be used except within the context of improvement projects. Sometimes, after all, it is possible to dismiss a highly useful idea simply because one feels it belongs to different contexts from those that are familiar or urgent in our classrooms.

We would like to urge teachers to take liberties rather than to apply formulas. Every classroom teacher knows that no single method, no matter how tried-and-true others may feel that it is, is going to provide *The Answer* when it comes to reaching the squirming minds that teachers face every day of their lives. Instead, learning relies on teachers' own creativity in establishing partnerships among a variety of learners, and in helping these young minds develop their own ways of grappling with problems and assessing alternatives.

Often, the improvement cycle is referred to within the context of problem solving. While it is not meant to address only *problems*, but areas of improvement opportunity as well, the problem-solving component of the process is fundamental to teachers' purposes in the classroom. That is, by helping students understand how to recognize and frame problems, formulate the appropriate questions, collect data in methodical ways, reflect on possibilities for improvement and trying these out in small ways, and ultimately changing processes and then re-examining them for possible further improvements, classroom teachers are equipping students with the kind of critical thinking skills that will prepare them to address the complex problems of life itself.

Teachers who want more help in using the improvement cycle in the classroom are referred to the bibliography at the end of this book. This short list is offered as a guide to further reading about various implications of what this guide for students has offered, including learning theory.

We would be pleased to discuss your applications or ideas for student use, or to share the stories that come out of your own classrooms, and we encourage you to contact us by phone or E-mail, through the publisher.

We acknowledge the suggestions and support of the reviewers of this work, including educational professionals and PQ Systems colleagues. We note the special contribution of Michael Wyatt Cleary to its completion.

A NOTE TO STUDENTS

You and your teacher want the same things for you. You want to do your best, and that's exactly what your parents and teachers want, too.

What does it mean to do your best?

Your best work does not just pop out by itself, as you know. It needs some help. You know when you have done work that is your very best, because you are proud of it and of what you have done to make it happen.

If you look back on things you did when you were younger, you know that you could probably do a better job with those tasks now, because you know more and have learned from lots of experiences that you've had. The birthday card that you made for your mother when you were only 5 years old may look childish and unfinished to you now. Since then, you have had lots of practice and you know you can make a birthday card that will look lots better now.

Your teachers don't expect you to do perfect work. They just want you to do the best you can, with the tools that you have right now.

So, doing your best work might mean the following:

- Understanding what task to do
- Knowing why you need to do the task
- Recognizing excellence for this task
- Having the right tools to do the task
- Knowing how to use those tools
- Completing the task on time
- Being proud of what you have accomplished
- Reviewing the task to see how it might have been done better
- Thinking about how this task helped you prepare for future tasks

Sometimes you work hard, but when you have finished your work, you know it is not as good as you might have done. Your teacher may think you didn't try hard enough, but you know you were trying as hard as you could.

Can you remember a time when you made something that didn't turn out as well as you thought it would? Write a story about that experience. If your teacher tells you that this book is yours to keep, you may write your paragraph here. If not, write it on another sheet of paper and keep it in your own thinking tools booklet that you will be making as you learn about some tools to help you do your best.

_____

_____

_____

_____

_____

_____

_____

_____

_____

_____

Your teacher will give you a chance to share this story with your classmates. This is a chance to talk about how you have already grown and learned since the first time you went to school or the days when you were younger.

This book will help you do your best work. It will also help you think about your best work. It will give you some ideas to make it easier to do work that you are proud of. It is based on many of the same ways that your teachers and principal work together to improve your school. To make things better in the school, they solve problems with some of the same tools you will learn in these pages.

These tools will help you improve your work. Some of them will improve a single task that you do (such as getting to school on time). More important, all of them are meant to help you think about what you do. When you think about what you do, you can make it better.

The book will also help you understand how important it is to look at all the facts. You will learn how to collect data. Then you will see how numbers or single facts can turn into information and understanding. Trying to change or improve something without having information is like building a cage for an animal when you have no idea how big it is.

If your teacher says it is all right to write in this book, use it like an activity book. The pages that are called "My Own Thinking Tools Page" can be copied for you to make your own book with these tools. Your book will have your own ideas as well as exercises to practice each tool. You may want to put the pages into a loose-leaf binder, or your teacher may have some ideas about bindings that will help you keep them together. When you are finished, you will have your own book. It will show what you have learned. You can refer to it later when you want to use one of these tools. Your own pages are your best learning.

Use these tools individually and together. Practice them at school and at home. They will become part of you, the same way that learning to read has become part of you. You will begin to think in a different way about solving problems.

And all of this will help you to do your best work. That's what everyone wants.

Please write to us, through the publisher, to tell us about your best work or how you improved your thinking practices or about things you learned when you were using these tools. We'd love to hear from you.

—Barbara A. Cleary
Sally J. Duncan

If you want to do this:	Gather as many ideas as you can	Group your ideas	Figure out how ideas connect	See the steps in something you do	Draw a picture of your data	Keep track of your facts
This tool may be useful:	Affinity exercise	Affinity exercise (chapter 2)	Fishbone diagram (chapter 2)	Flowchart (chapter 7) (chapter 4)	Histogram (chapter 8)	Check sheet (chapter 6)
	Brainstorming (chapter 1)	Fishbone diagram (chapter 4)	Relations diagram (chapter 5)		Line graph (chapter 9)	Line graph (chapter 9)
	Lotus flower diagram (chapter 3)	Lotus flower diagram (chapter 3)			Pareto diagram (chapter 10)	

FIGURE I.2. Matrix for suggested use of tools

xviii

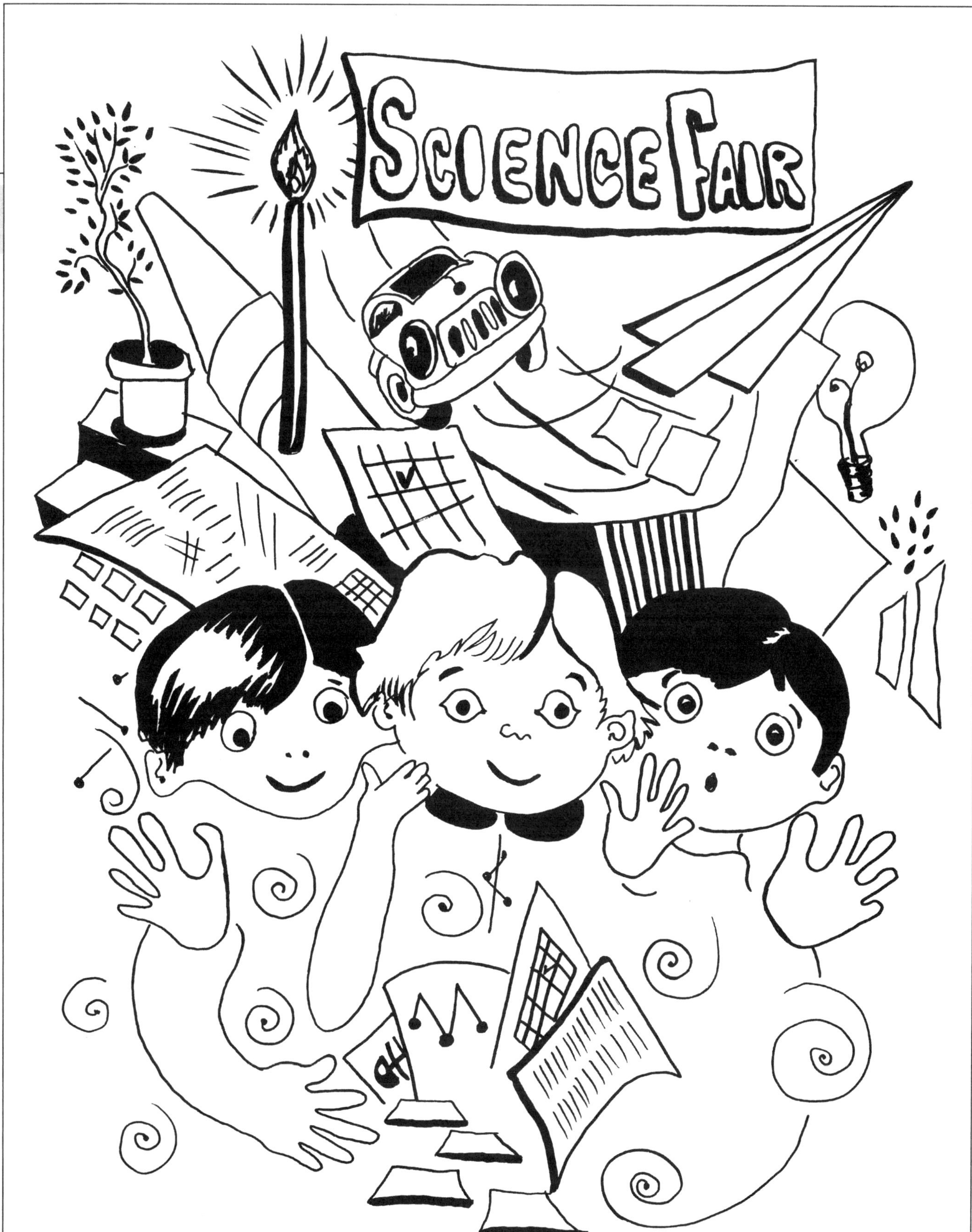
SCIENCE FAIR

SECTION 1

TOOLS FOR COLLECTING IDEAS

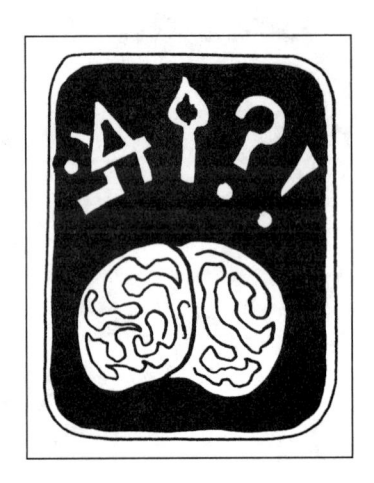

CHAPTER 1

BRAINSTORMING
Digging for New Ideas

Madison had worked all by herself on her school's science fair project. She was as proud of this fact as she was of her entry. Her project was a way to light a wooden match without having to strike it. To do this, she clipped the match to a small truck that ran down a track, gaining momentum as it moved. When it got to the bottom of the track, it went under a block of wood with sandpaper glued to it. The match, rubbing against the sandpaper, burst into flame.

Madison thought it was a clever way to light a match. She practiced running the truck down the track over and over, making sure it would make contact with the sandpaper. She did not show the experiment to Ms. Chadwick, her teacher, before the fair. Instead, she told Ms. Chadwick in general terms about the purpose of her experiment—to start a fire with an automatic process. She was vague about it, even though her teacher pressed her to write out the details of the project. Madison was proud of the fact that she had done the whole thing herself, from thinking it up to putting all the parts together. She had not shared it with anyone. She liked the fact that it was a kind of secret.

When she got to the gym where the science fair was held, Madison started setting up her project. As she looked around, she saw other students' projects. They were far more complicated than hers. They involved animals or plants or other living things, and nearly all of them were the work of several students together, rather than just one. "At least I did this all by myself," she thought. She knew there was no chance that it would fail.

Taking the parts of her project out of the box, she was stunned to find that she had forgotten the matches that were a part of the setup. She must have left them on her desk when she was packing things to take to the fair. Panicked, she went through everything again. Then she ran from table to table, asking other students if they had matches. Finally, a boy with a Bunsen burner gave her a handful of wooden matches for her project. Relieved, Madison went back to her area to finish getting ready. She attached the match to the clip on top of the little truck, put up her sign that explained the project, and stood ready for the judges. "Wait till they see my match light," she thought.

Two teachers with clipboards walked up to Madison's table where the experiment was set up. She explained its purpose to them. She also mentioned that she had made the project all by herself. When they were ready, she gave the truck a little push down the track, on its way to light the match and finish the project. The judges' eyes moved down the track as the truck curved and dropped, gaining speed for the final step. When it got to the sandpaper block, however, it flew right under it without making contact. The match did not light, and the truck dropped onto the floor with the unlit match still clipped to its roof.

What had gone wrong? Madison could not believe that the match had not lit. It was the same experiment that she had practiced over and over at home. The judges moved on to the next table, jotting notes on their clipboards. Madison waited until the other projects had been evaluated and prizes had been given. Then she packed her things up and sadly walked home.

When she looked at the matches that she had used for the science fair, she saw that they were almost half an inch shorter than the ones she had originally used. When her classmate had given her the matches, she had been so relieved that she had not thought of this. Because the match was too short, it did not reach the sandpaper block or make contact in order to light. "How careless of me," she cried. How had she forgotten what she needed to take to the science fair? If the matches had been the right size, her experiment would have worked perfectly and the judges would have been impressed, she knew.

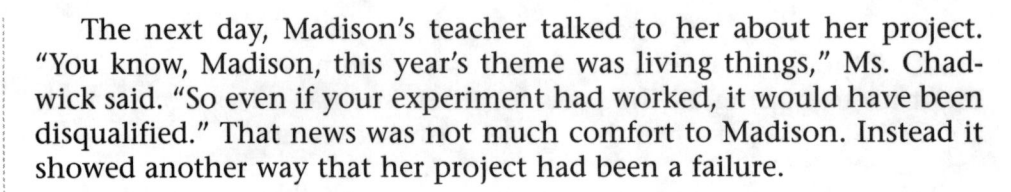

The next day, Madison's teacher talked to her about her project. "You know, Madison, this year's theme was living things," Ms. Chadwick said. "So even if your experiment had worked, it would have been disqualified." That news was not much comfort to Madison. Instead it showed another way that her project had been a failure.

Ms. Chadwick told her that when they had first heard about the science fair, the other students had gotten together in small groups to brainstorm about some ideas for projects that they could do together. Because Madison had not decided to enter her project until much later than the others, she had not participated in this brainstorming. Instead, she was on her own. As teams worked on their projects, they gave each other suggestions or reminded themselves of things they needed to remember. Because none of them knew what Madison was doing, they could not support her with their ideas or offer suggestions about how to improve her project. There was no one on her team, after all.

"You know, Madison, sometimes the thinking of three or four people is much better than the thinking of just one," her teacher said.

"Isn't that cheating?" Madison asked.

"No," Ms. Chadwick said. "Each team came up with an original idea. The brainstorming helped them to get started and to think of things that might work. They worked together as teams, rather than as individuals." Madison knew that the rules allowed both team entries and individual projects.

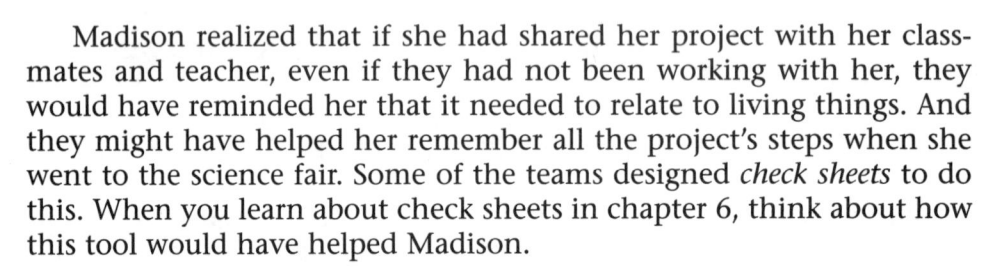

Madison realized that if she had shared her project with her classmates and teacher, even if they had not been working with her, they would have reminded her that it needed to relate to living things. And they might have helped her remember all the project's steps when she went to the science fair. Some of the teams designed *check sheets* to do this. When you learn about check sheets in chapter 6, think about how this tool would have helped Madison.

Madison discovered that even when one does her own work, that work can benefit from the ideas of others. "I guess I won't be so secretive about my project next time," she decided. She had learned more about solving problems than about lighting matches the hard way.

Madison's classmates had engaged in *brainstorming*, a tool that helps to generate lots of ideas. They used brainstorming to create ideas for projects. Brainstorming has many other uses, too.

To brainstorm, a group of people forms a circle so everyone can see everyone else. They begin with one person's first idea. Someone writes all the ideas on the board or on a large sheet of paper so everyone can see them. Going around the circle, everyone gives an idea.

If a group member does not have an idea at that moment, he or she should say "pass" for that round. The same person may have an idea in the next round, and can say it then. Someone else's idea can sometimes spark a new thought. When one idea helps someone else think of another one, this is sometimes called *hitchhiking* or *piggy-backing*. Example: If someone says "grow lima beans," this idea might cause someone else to say, "compare different growing conditions for lima beans." Hitchhiking should be encouraged, because it helps generate even more ideas.

The purpose of brainstorming is to come up with as many ideas as possible. Group members should make no comment about ideas when they are said. Whether they are good or bad, they are ideas to be considered. Sometimes an idea may seem really strange, but it can help others in the group to think of another idea. No one's ideas should be shut down by another group member's comment or body language. Everyone's thinking should be considered in brainstorming.

A brainstorming list for a science fair project might include the following ideas:

1. Making a rocket
2. Growing avocados from seeds
3. Measuring growth of plants in light and dark conditions
4. Breeding fruit flies

5. Testing effect of chemicals on plants
6. Making a bridge out of balsam sticks
7. Designing a greenhouse
8. Training mice in mazes
9. Finding a cure for colds
10. Measuring growth of birds with different feed
11. Training a monkey to type
12. Building a laser table
13. Comparing boiling points of liquids
14. Testing the strength of various vines
15. Checking people's eyesight in light and dark conditions
16. Lowering blood pressure
17. Finding a way to measure body fat
18. Experimenting with gerbil diets

Finally, after no one has anything else to add to the list, the brainstorming will stop. Everyone should look at the list and be sure that each idea is clear. This is the time to ask questions if someone does not understand something. It is not the time to criticize or cross ideas off the list, though. Remember that everyone's ideas are valuable at this point.

The main goal of brainstorming is to get ideas from *everyone*, not just those who like to talk. These ideas can be used in a variety of ways. Sometimes, the brainstorming list is used with another tool. For example, if you brainstorm about gifts for your family, you may want to use this list for an affinity exercise (chapter 2). This tool will help you to group or classify the ideas. You will learn about other tools in other chapters. Try to think of ways to combine the tools as you learn about them in this book.

NARROWING THE LIST DOWN

Sometimes it is enough just to get lots of ideas about something. Usually, though, you will want to narrow the list down. You will probably want to pick only one science project, for example. This may be easy, especially if your group agrees immediately or if you are working by yourself from the suggestions that everyone has made. The science project idea can be simply the one you like best.

When you do need to pick only one or two ideas from this list, take the next step, called *nominal group technique*. This means first deciding on criteria, or rules, for picking items from a brainstorm list. For example, one rule for selecting a science project is that it must relate to living things. Every idea that does not have something to do with living things can be crossed off the list. Other rules, or criteria, for the science project might include the following:

1. It must be portable.
2. It cannot cost more than $25 to make.
3. It should be easy for one person to demonstrate.
4. It should be something that has not been entered before.

The team can apply these criteria to its list, crossing off things that do not pass these rules. Any ideas that are not crossed off can be discussed further. The final step in the nominal group technique is to take a preliminary vote.

Nominal group technique is better than simple voting because it helps groups to come to consensus. This means that everyone can accept an idea even if it is not his or her favorite. With regular voting, one idea "wins," and others "lose." This makes members of a team feel that they may not be able to accept the winning idea if it was not their own. To enhance teamwork, the nominal group technique is preferred.

Preliminary ranking starts by having each person select the top ideas that he or she prefers. If the list of items is longer than twenty, select eight; for shorter lists, five or six ideas are usually enough. The items on the original list should be numbered, so they can be referred to by number as well as by what they are. Each person should write each idea that he or she has chosen on a separate 3 × 5 card, shown in Figure 1.1. Each should spread his or her cards out on the table, to be able to see them and think about preferences.

FIGURE 1.1 Card for ranking items

All members of the group should spread their cards out in front of themselves in this way. They begin by choosing the most important or most preferred idea, and give this a rank of 5, if they will be selecting five ideas. (For four ideas, give the favorite a 4.) Notice that the most preferred idea has the greatest number. It is *not* ranked with a 1 to show that it is first, but with a 5 to show that it gets five of that person's votes. One way to think of this is to imagine that you are *voting* with gumdrops. You would give the most gumdrops to your favorite idea. Write the rank in the lower right corner of your card.

Each person chooses the next most important and gives it a rank of 4 (four gumdrops!). Then each of the next most preferred ideas is ranked, from 3 down to 1. The least important of the five chosen receives a 1, but of course it is still on the list of the top five. The cards are given to the group leader, who writes all the rankings on the original brainstorming list. They are not added together. Instead, each ranking is written, as Figure 1.2 shows.

The group discusses the outcome of the vote. Some items will have no support. The ones with the most numbers, and the highest numbers, are considered. "Training mice in mazes," for example, has more numbers than the others, with 8. It does not have the greatest number of 5 votes, however. "Experimenting with gerbil diets" has three 5s and two 4s, while "Training mice in mazes" has only two 5s and two 4s. The group should focus on these two items. The mice idea has the highest ranking, since it has more votes (eight rather than five).

Everyone in the group must be able to accept the idea that is selected. If not, further discussion should take place, and even another vote if necessary. Talking about these two ideas might bring the suggestion that they could be combined. If the group finds this to be an acceptable approach, they will select the combined ideas. If everything else is eliminated, and another vote is taken, one of the two ideas may have a clearly higher rank.

The item with the highest ranking of all the items on the list is the one that has the group's consensus, or general support. This is the one that the team has selected. In the case of the science fair, this is the project that the team will work on together. More discussion may be needed, either to refine the original idea or to be sure that there is consensus.

Brainstorming can be used to come up with plans and projects. It can also help with problem-solving and improvement efforts. Whenever you want to generate lots of ideas, brainstorming is the way to go. The nominal group technique is a way to select from the list of ideas that have been created.

1. Making a rocket
2. Growing avocados from seeds 5-5-3-1
3. Measuring growth of plants in light and dark conditions 4-3-3-1
4. Breeding fruit flies 1-2-2-4-5-4
5. Testing effect of chemicals on plants
6. Making a bridge out of balsam sticks
7. Designing a greenhouse 3-3-4-1-1-1
8. Training mice in mazes 5-5-4-3-4-2-2-2
9. Finding a cure for colds
10. Measuring growth of birds with different feed 2-2-3
11. Training a monkey to type 1-1-2
12. Building a laser table
13. Comparing boiling points of liquids
14. Testing the strength of various vines 4-5-4-3-2
15. Checking people's eyesight in light and dark conditions 2-2
16. Lowering blood pressure
17. Finding a way to measure body fat 3-2-2
18. Experimenting with gerbil diets 4-5-5-4-5

FIGURE 1.2 List with rankings

training mice in mazes

FIGURE 1.3 Crawford slip for science project

VARIATION: THE CRAWFORD SLIP METHOD

Sometimes, when there is a sensitive issue, people may not want to say their ideas aloud. Or there may be so many people that it would take forever for everyone to express ideas individually.

A different kind of brainstorming involves writing rather than saying ideas. This is called the Crawford slip method. Instead of going around the circle and having everyone say their ideas aloud, the Crawford slip method uses slips of paper or sticky notes. Each idea is written on a separate slip of paper. The ideas for the science fair would be written like the one in Figure 1.3. Notice that it is similar to the small slip that was used for ranking. This slip, though, has no number and no rank. It is just a way to write down an idea. Each idea must be on a separate slip or card so all ideas can be analyzed when everyone is finished.

SUGGESTIONS FOR USING BRAINSTORMING

- Whenever you need lots of ideas, consider brainstorming techniques.
- Give plenty of time for everyone to think of ideas *before the brainstorming begins* as well as during the brainstorming.
- Be sure that everyone has an opportunity to express ideas without criticism.
- Keep the original list in case you need to come back to these ideas again. You may try something and find that it does not work, and you may want to go back to your original thinking.

OTHER TOOLS YOU MAY USE WITH BRAINSTORMING

- Affinity exercise, to group your ideas after brainstorming

- Fishbone diagrams to generate possible causes

- Pareto charts, for groups that can be counted and then shown in a Pareto chart

- Histograms, similar to Pareto charts (chapter 8)

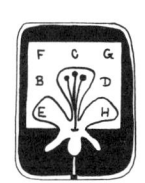

- Lotus flower diagrams, to develop ideas for the center square (chapter 3)

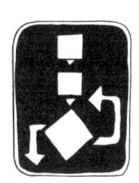

- Flowcharts, to be sure no steps are forgotten (chapter 7)

NAME: _____

CLASS: _____

DATE: _____

MY OWN THINKING TOOLS PAGE
BRAINSTORMING

First, Some Practice

In your classroom, form a small group with three to four other students. Practice the rules of brainstorming by using them for one of the items on the list that follows. If you have several different groups in your class, be sure that they all select different topics from the list provided. If you prefer, decide your own topic for brainstorming rather than using this list. It is meant to help you get started, but if there is something else that is more useful for your class, please choose that instead.

First, simply come up with a list of ideas by having everyone in your small group share ideas one at a time. Before you begin brainstorming, select one person in your group to be the facilitator. This person will write all the ideas on the board or on a large sheet of paper.

1. Ways you can spend a gift of $100 that the parents' organization gave to your class this year
2. How you can get out of your classroom in the event of a fire if the main doorway is blocked
3. How you can save time during the day so you can add it to your recess
4. Some things you can do to reduce noise in the hallways
5. How you could teach yourselves for a day if your teacher were absent and there were no substitute teacher
6. Kinds of assembly programs you'd like to have
7. Visitors you'd like to invite to your classroom
8. Ways to create more space for quiet reading in your classroom
9. How you can celebrate everyone's birthdays in a fair and equal way
10. Ways to have more time for art in the day's schedule
11. Ideas for developing a class newspaper
12. How to improve the care of our classroom gerbil or fish
13. How to improve our spelling

When you have gotten everyone's ideas, do the next steps in brainstorming. Using the same facilitator, decide what your *selection criteria* will be. Then do preliminary ranking to select an item that everyone in your group can accept.

After all the groups have finished with their brainstorming and ranking processes, share your outcomes with the class as a whole. What did you learn about brainstorming? How did you feel about sharing your ideas with this tool? Write your response here, and then share these with your group:

_____

_____

_____

_____

Now It's Your Turn...

You may already be working in groups for some other purpose in your classroom. These might be reading groups, science project groups, or other kinds of groups. If so, meet with these teams to do brainstorming. If you do not have such groups, organize into teams with particular interests or shared activities (a hobby, for example, or a movie that you've seen together, or the same number of brothers and sisters in your family).

Decide on four or five different areas in which you might brainstorm ideas for improvement or an activity. Write these areas below:

1. _____

2. _____

3. _____

4. _____

5. _____

Using the same methods you used above, brainstorm about one of these topics. Pick someone to be your facilitator, and follow the rules for brainstorming.

HOME CONNECTION

At home, you will probably be able to think of lots of ways you can use brainstorming. You can teach your family the rules and then use the tool to solve problems, improve situations that you face, and plan for future events. You will find that it reduces the amount of bickering among members of your family. It will also help everyone to feel that his or her ideas have been heard. Brainstorming promotes a feeling of fairness.

Try using some of the following topics for brainstorming with your family. After you have used one of these topics, you can use the tool to brainstorm about other areas where you can use it.

1. Ways to decide tasks around the house
2. Where to go on vacation
3. A family activity for the weekend
4. How to be sure the back gate is always locked
5. Ways to deliver telephone messages for family members
6. Meals for this week
7. Ways to create more space in the garage (or elsewhere)
8. How we can celebrate birthdays in our family
9. How our family can give service to others
10. What we can do to increase allowances

NAME: _____

CLASS: _____

DATE: _____

BRAINSTORMING LIST

Topic: _____

Ideas:

1. _____
2. _____
3. _____
4. _____
5. _____
6. _____
7. _____
8. _____
9. _____
10. _____
11. _____
12. _____
13. _____
14. _____
15. _____
16. _____
17. _____
18. _____
19. _____
20. _____
21. _____
22. _____
23. _____
24. _____
25. _____
26. _____
27. _____
28. _____

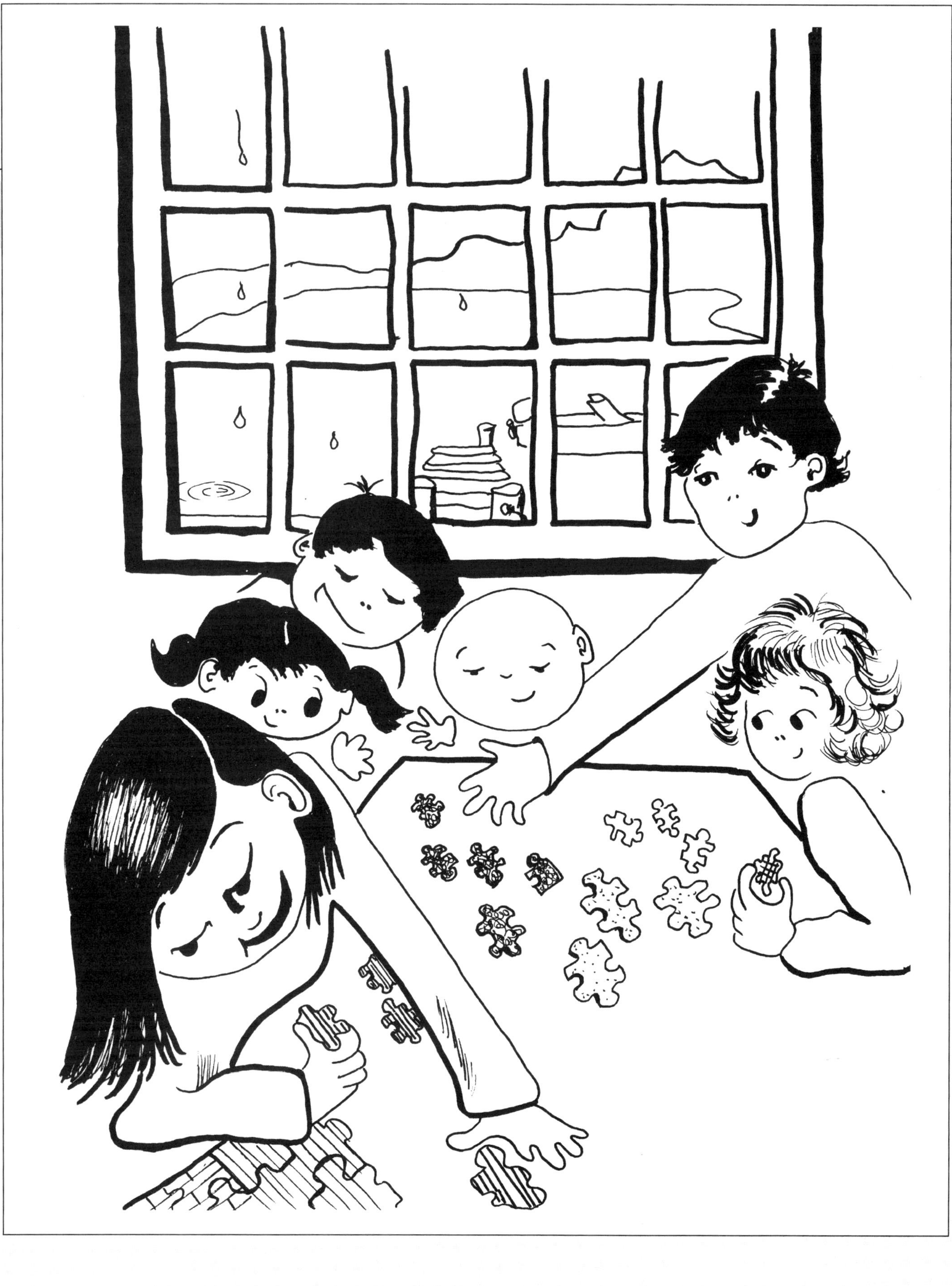

CHAPTER 2

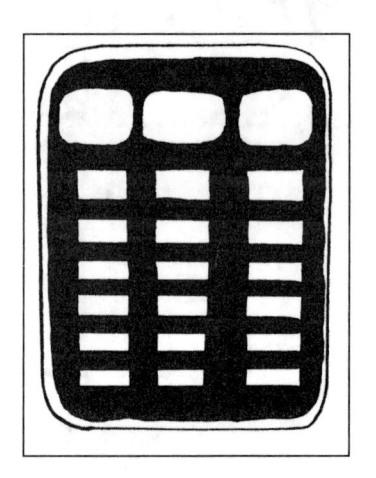

AFFINITY EXERCISES
Putting Things in Their Places

Twins Charlie and Emma were looking forward to their vacation at the lake. Every summer they went to their aunt and uncle's cabin for 2 weeks. They went canoeing and sailing and swam at the beach. They also played games with their cousins Tracy, Terry, and Tommy. Except for the summer visit, they rarely saw their cousins, so they were especially excited about being with them. Besides, their parents had promised that they could try waterskiing. Charlie and Emma had become good swimmers and were big enough to handle the tow ropes. This was going to be a great vacation.

Charlie and Emma had never been on a vacation that was not a visit to relatives. They thought that having lots of family members around was what vacation was about. Their dad said it was a less expensive way to see another place. They thought it was the best vacation they could have, even if they paid lots more for one.

On the first day at the lake, they helped their parents put the dock into the water. They also blew up the rubber rafts and launched the boat. It was a beautiful, sunny day. They went to sleep that night eager to start their waterskiing lessons in the morning.

Jumping out of bed the next day, however, they found that the sunny skies had turned gray. A steady, heavy rain was beating on the metal roof of the cabin. Wind banged the boat against the dock. The cabin was damp and cold as they padded around in their bare feet looking sadly out the windows. "Waterskiing will have to wait till tomorrow," Aunt Laura said. They sighed, hoping that the rain would let up and they would be able to go in the boat as they had planned.

Charlie and Emma tried to read their books for awhile. It was hard to think. Tommy and Tracy kept running to the front windows to report that it was still raining. They all began to tease and bother each other. Soon Tracy was in tears. This was going to be a long day. It was, after all, a very small cabin.

Then Charlie and Emma's older brother Ross built a fire in the fireplace. The cabin was quite cozy. If it were not for the disappointment over their waterskiing plans, they would have enjoyed being cooped up by the weather. Now, though, they were all restless and a little cross.

Finally Uncle Tim suggested that they sit down and do a jigsaw puzzle. Happy to find a way to lessen their boredom, Charlie and Emma, Ross, and the cousins all gathered with the adults to begin. This puzzle looked hard because of all the pieces that it had, clumped together in a plastic bag. Because the box had been lost, they had no picture of what it would look like when they finished. "This is impossible," Charlie said.

Uncle Tim said that they would just have to organize the parts. Without the box, they would sort the pieces. Then they would decide what each group of pieces might be. Terry had done the puzzle once before, so she remembered that it was a picture of a country village. It had several small buildings and some kind of town square in the middle. "Let's each take a color or a pattern and gather all the pieces that look the same," Uncle Tim suggested.

What they were doing was a kind of *affinity exercise,* a grouping tool. That is, they were sorting puzzle pieces according to the ways they were alike. This is an easy way to sort things. If you think of things in your house that have been sorted, you may see the same idea. Socks are kept in one drawer, and jeans or shirts are kept in another. This helps you find your clothes without having to look through every drawer. Like the puzzle, the drawers can be seen as an affinity sorting, with things that are similar kept together.

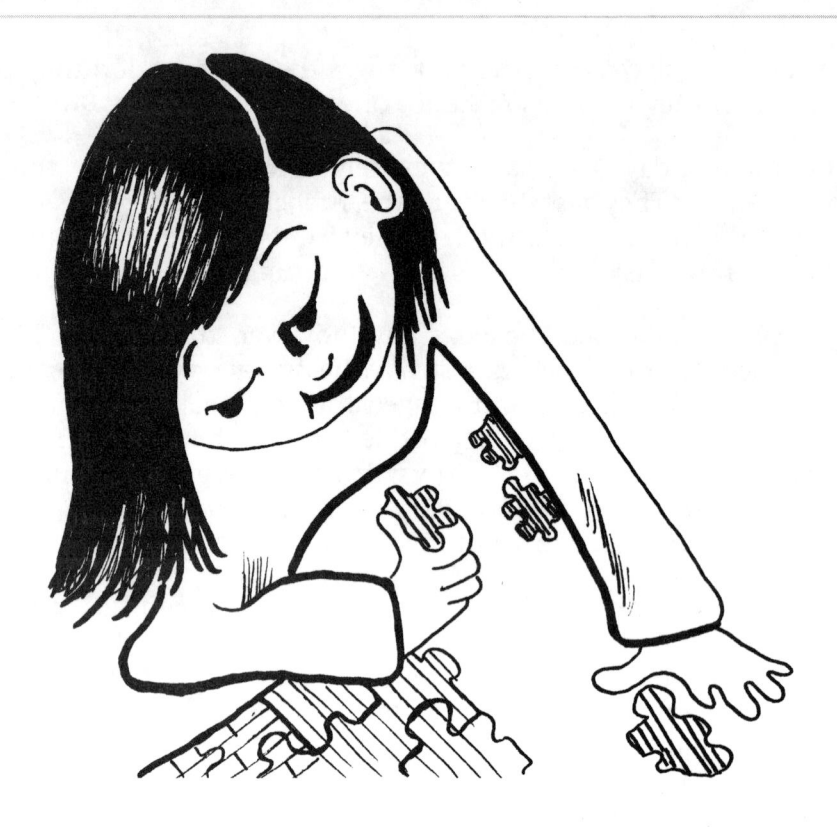

Affinity exercises can also be used to sort *ideas*, rather than *things* like puzzle pieces. Sometimes you need to make ideas clear so you can think about them. Sorting them and seeing what they have in common is one way to do this.

The biggest group of puzzle pieces was made up of various kinds of red tiles. These must be roofs of houses and other buildings, they thought. The reason for sorting the pieces was not to find the largest group. It was to separate and sort all the pieces. Then they could be put together into a whole puzzle.

Here's an example of using an affinity exercise to organize ideas, instead of things:

A group of young people wanted to plan a parade and picnic for their neighborhood to celebrate the Fourth of July. They began by thinking of ideas about the event. They tried to think of everything that should be part of the day's activities. They asked, "What should be a part of the celebration?"

Everybody then wrote ideas on small slips of paper. This is a kind of written *brainstorming* known as the Crawford slip method, as you learned in chapter 1. All you need to do is write one idea per slip of paper. Keep writing until all your ideas have been recorded.

When the Fourth of July group had all finished writing their ideas, they spread the small slips of paper out on a table, so they could see all

What should be included in the celebration?

children's floats	hot dogs	5-K run
music	flags	hot air balloon rides
food	honor guard	games for little kids
homemade ice cream	pet contest	volleyball
bicycle decorating	eating watermelon	bike parade
wagon decorating	tug of war	lawnmower parade
bands	water balloons	pie eating contest
parade queen	three-legged race	

FIGURE 2.1 Fourth of July brainstorming

Food	Parade ideas	Games	Other activities
homemade ice cream	children's floats	three-legged race	music
hot dogs	bicycle decorating	tug of war	pet contest
food	wagon decorating	water balloons	hot air balloon rides
pie eating contest	bands	games for little kids	5-K run
eating watermelon	parade queen	volleyball	pie eating contest
	honor guard		
	flags		
	bike parade		
	lawnmower parade		

FIGURE 2.2 Fourth of July affinity exercise

of them. Then they began to place them into groups of ideas that were similar in some way. The ideas included those in Figure 2.1.

They organized the ideas into groups, in the same way that Charlie and Emma had organized their puzzle pieces. Figure 2.2 shows how the affinity diagram looked.

The planners were then able to look at the groups. They could decide which ones should be included in the celebration. After that, they decided which of the ideas were things they actually wanted to do. Some of the ideas they could not do by themselves, like "hot air balloon rides." They cut this from the list.

Like Charlie and Emma's jigsaw puzzle, the various parts were finally connected. Each one added something to the event as a whole. All of the parts were there. Because they had been organized around a single idea, they seemed to fit together better. The planners felt that nothing they wanted had been left out. They also had a chance to leave out some of the weaker ideas that did not seem to add anything to the celebration.

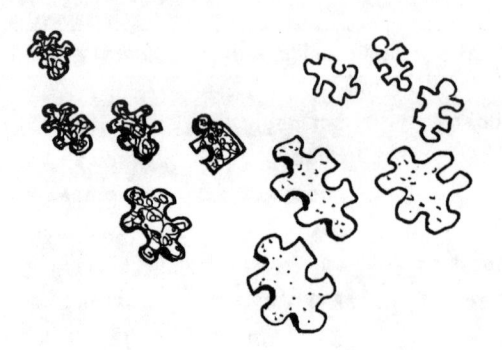

The affinity diagram helped the group of children organize their ideas and look ahead to the celebration. Without a tool like this one, sometimes people think of good ideas too late to put them into effect. Thinking something through before doing it is always a good idea. Affinity exercises help people do this.

SUGGESTIONS FOR USING THE AFFINITY EXERCISE

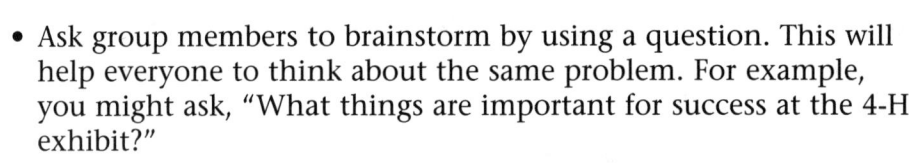

- Ask group members to brainstorm by using a question. This will help everyone to think about the same problem. For example, you might ask, "What things are important for success at the 4-H exhibit?"
- Be sure that everyone has a chance to record all ideas. Sometimes group members need time to think, so be sure the process is not too fast.
- Only one idea should be written on each slip of paper. Sometimes sticky notes are better, but any small pieces of paper can be used.
- After the ideas have been put into groups, be sure to let people look them over. People might think of new ideas when they see the groups. Be ready to add these to the groups where they belong.
- Remember that many of the ideas may not be used at all. Nonetheless, everyone should be as creative as possible while they are thinking of ideas.

OTHER TOOLS YOU MAY USE WITH THE AFFINITY EXERCISE

You will be learning about other tools in this book. As you do, think about ways that the tools can be used together. You may want to look back at the matrix in the introduction (see Figure I.2). There, you will see that there may be more than one tool to use for a particular purpose. Some tools that you may find yourself using along with affinity exercises include:

- Brainstorming, including the Crawford slip method

- Pareto charts, if the group is interested in seeing which idea is mentioned most often

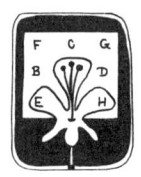

- Lotus flower diagrams to help people think more about any of the ideas or groups that pop up in the affinity exercise

- Check sheets, to help keep track of ideas as they are used

- Relations diagrams, to help show connections among the affinity items

NAME: _____

CLASS: _____

DATE: _____

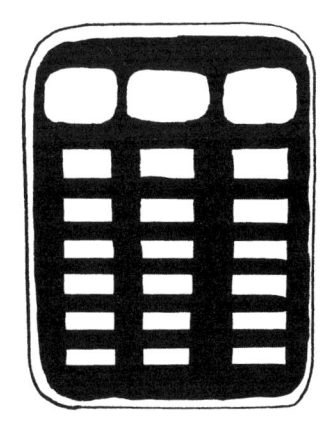

MY OWN THINKING TOOLS PAGE
AFFINITY EXERCISE

First, Some Practice

For fun, you may want to start by doing a puzzle, like Charlie and Emma did. You will see that certain puzzle pieces seem to go together even before you know exactly what they are. Group the puzzle pieces by color or type (edge or middle, for example) before you try to put the puzzle together.

Now let's try to group ideas, rather than puzzle pieces. Organize the following list of items by using an affinity exercise. First, find ways in which items are similar. Then create separate categories that include only items that are alike in some way. You may want to cut out the words (if this is your copy of the activity book) and put them into piles of similar objects. You may also identify similar items by using different marks. For example, you could circle all the items that represent the first category, and underline those in the second category, and so on.

elephant	rain	paper clip	scissors
map	orange juice	eucalyptus tree	ruler
hamburger	frozen yogurt	baby gerbils	cocker spaniel
dictionary	clock	carrots	boa constrictor
platypus	milkshake	crayons	tomato juice
dill pickles	salamander	white glue	popcorn

The affinity exercise begins with brainstorming, not with a chart to record ideas. It is important to think of ideas, rather than of groups, as you begin the exercise. It is only after you have come up with a list of ideas that you will name the ways that they are similar.

Now that you have a list of ideas (above), study the affinity chart in Figure 2.3. On this chart, you can see that the groups have been named: *food, animals,* and *objects.*

1. Food	2. Animals	3. Objects
hamburger	platypus	_____
dill pickles	_____	_____
orange juice	_____	_____
frozen yogurt	_____	_____
milkshake	_____	_____
carrots	_____	_____
tomato juice	_____	_____
popcorn	_____	_____

FIGURE 2.3 Affinity chart

The first list is nearly complete. Finish the chart by completing the lists for the other categories.

You have separated the items so they can be seen as distinct groups. List some advantages to seeing the names of the items in different categories rather than all together on the same list:

1. _____

2. _____

3. _____

4. _____

Now It's Your Turn...

When you use the affinity exercise to organize *ideas* rather than *things*, there are even more advantages. Try this in a small group or with a partner. This time, you will generate your own ideas, rather than beginning with a list of items that someone else has thought of for you.

Using silent brainstorming, think of as many different ways as possible to celebrate Thanksgiving in your classroom.

Ask your group to write these down on sticky notes or small pieces of paper as they think of ideas. Do not criticize or praise the ideas at this point. Wait until all of the members of your group have had a chance to give all of their ideas. Then spread all the sticky notes on a table or put them on the wall so everyone can see them. How can the ideas be classified into categories that are similar?

After the groups have been created, write the *headers,* or the names of the groups, on the top lines of each group, below. Use as many different categories (or boxes) as you need to cover all of the ideas. If you find some items that do not seem to fit into any other categories, you may identify one header as *miscellaneous.*

1 _____ 2 _____ 3 _____

   _____   _____   _____
   _____   _____   _____
   _____   _____   _____
   _____   _____   _____
   _____   _____   _____
   _____   _____   _____
   _____   _____   _____

4 _____ 5 _____ 6 _____

   _____   _____   _____
   _____   _____   _____
   _____   _____   _____
   _____   _____   _____
   _____   _____   _____
   _____   _____   _____
   _____   _____   _____

You have organized a list of ideas. The affinity exercise helps you think about items on the list and what they have in common. You have put like items together, and moved unlike items to other categories. This helps you focus on groups of ideas before you look at separate, individual ideas.

Try using the affinity exercise for a class activity. Here are some ideas, but you can think of some as well. Your teacher may have some ideas about exercises that are related to something you are studying.

1. Plan an event. This can be something simple like a birthday celebration for your teacher or a more complex school event.
2. Organize ideas presented in your classroom. For example, by asking "What are the most important ideas in this chapter?" you can make a list that may

include isolated facts as well as important concepts. The affinity exercise will help you put these into contexts so you can be sure of what you have learned.

You are recognizing the patterns that ideas have. For example, if the chapter tells you about different inventions, you may be able to group these under the names of the inventors. Other ways to sort them might include places where they were invented, the time periods in which they were invented, or kinds of inventions. "Thomas Edison," "1884," and "New Jersey" are isolated facts or data until you are able to put them together around a single idea. They are all related to the invention of the lightbulb.

3. Picture yourself winning your next athletic or fine arts contest. Use an affinity exercise to generate and organize ideas about what can bring about its success.

In your group, discuss the ways that this tool has helped you to organize your ideas, without interfering with creative thinking. If you had started the process with the headers, rather than generating ideas first, how would this have made the final outcome different?

A completed affinity diagram will have both headers (or categories) and items in the group. The last page of this chapter shows a pattern that an affinity diagram may have. Remember, however, that since you begin with ideas, rather than groups, each individual affinity diagram will be different from all other affinity diagrams.

HOME CONNECTION

After you have practiced using affinity exercises at school, tell your family about them and teach them how to organize things or ideas with this tool. Here are some ideas for you to try at home:

1. Organize items that need to be taken on a trip, a picnic, or to school, to be sure nothing is forgotten.
2. Brainstorm about gifts for members of your family and group your ideas with an affinity diagram.
3. Plan your family vacation by thinking of all the things you would like to do together. Group them with an affinity diagram so you can decide which activities you will do.
4. Use an affinity exercise to sort all the things in your basement or attic. Group similar items together and plan the space by looking at these groups.

NAME: _____

CLASS: _____

DATE: _____

AFFINITY DIAGRAM TEMPLATE

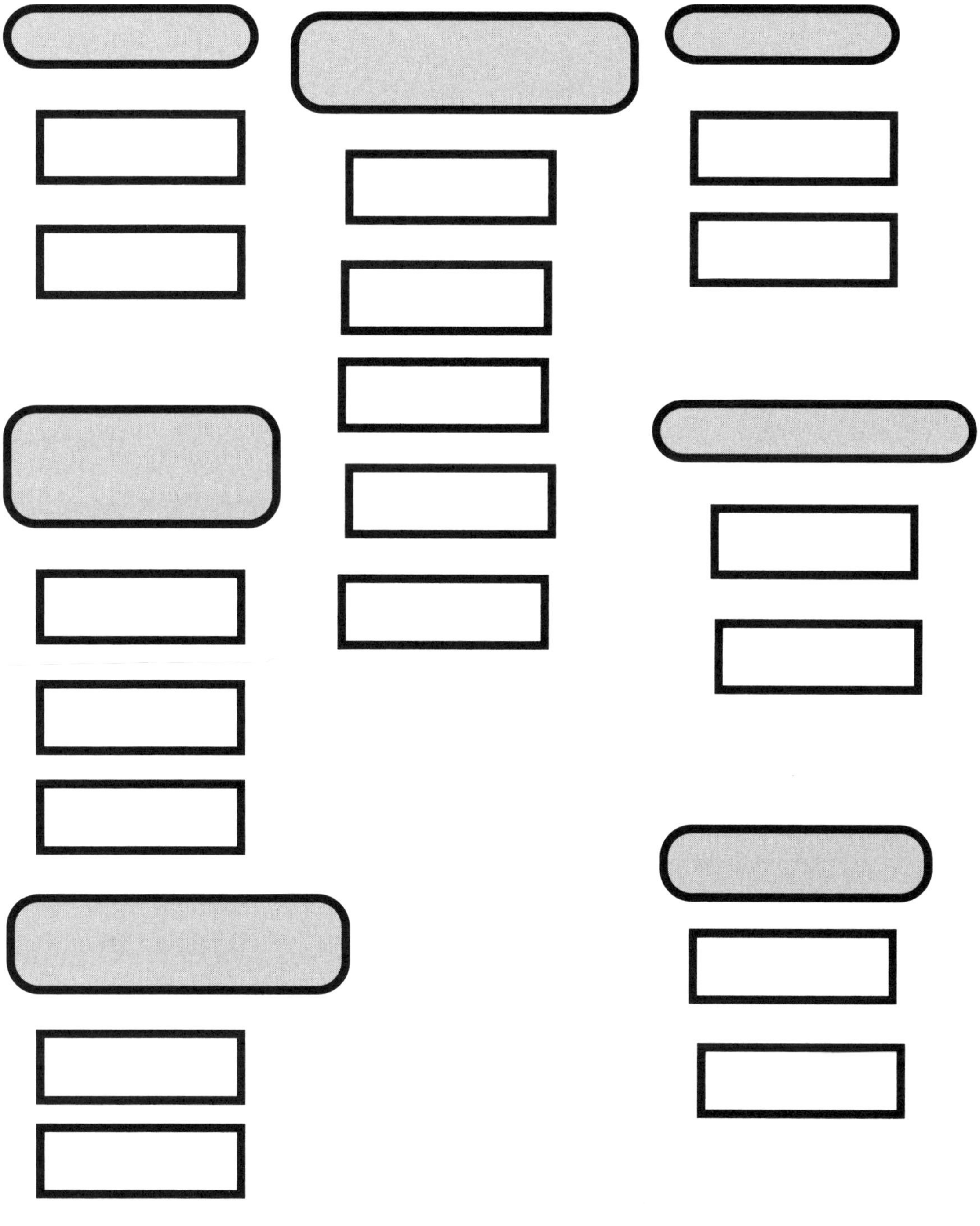

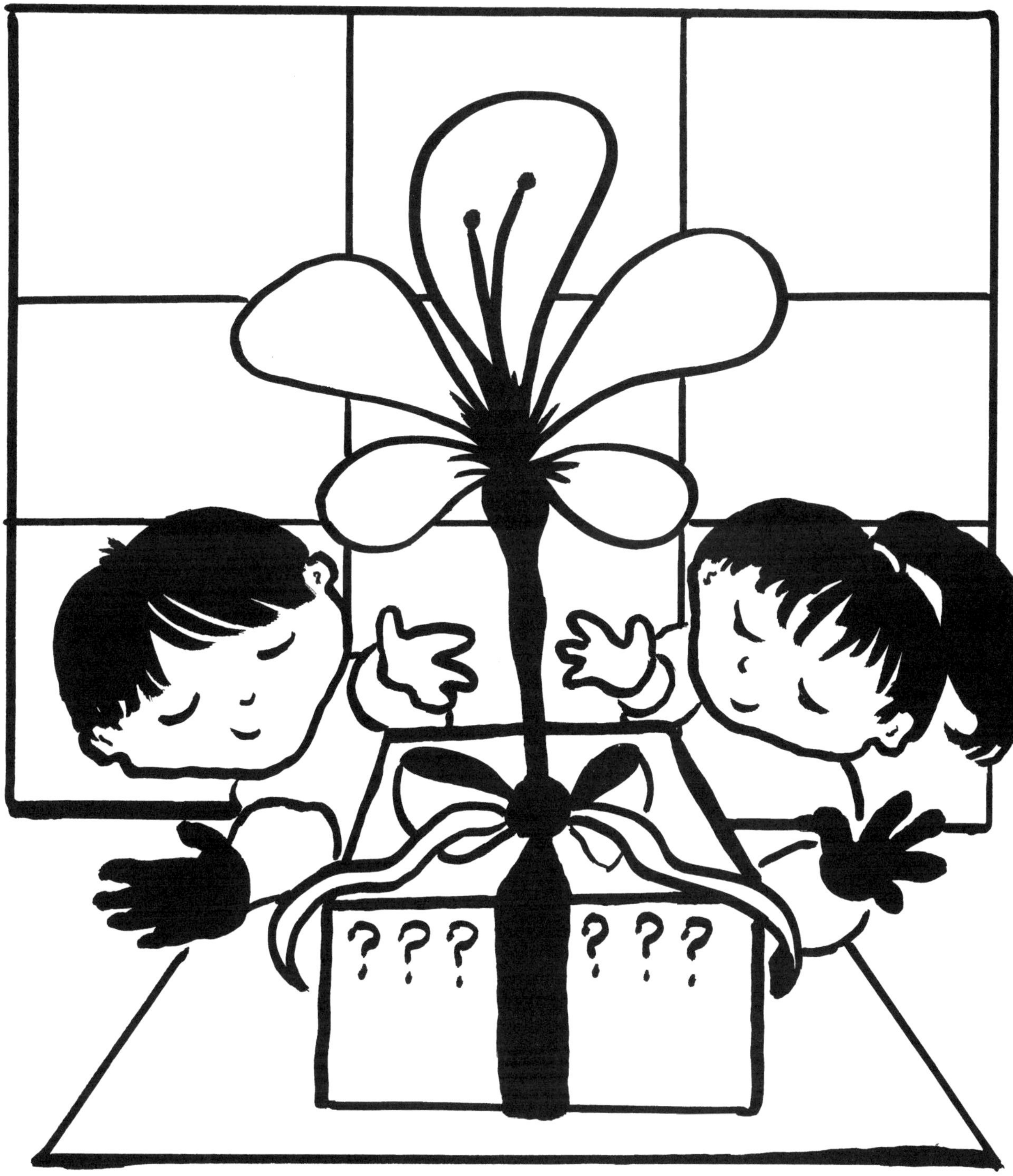

CHAPTER 3

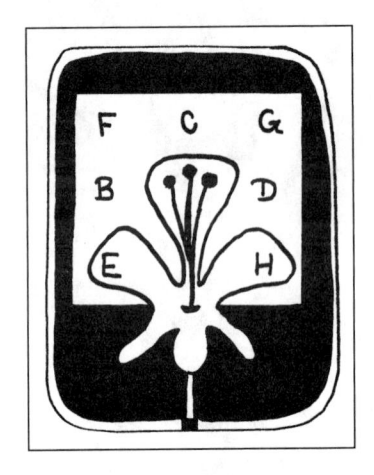

LOTUS FLOWER DIAGRAMS

Blossoming with New Ideas

Jake and Rebecca spent 2 weeks of their summer vacation with their grandmother in New Jersey. Now they wanted to give her something special for her birthday. They also wanted to show their appreciation for the wonderful visit they had had with her.

Before, the two had always gone shopping for gifts with their mother. She helped them to pick something out for Nana. Sometimes, they ended up arguing at the store because they could not agree on a gift. Other years, they had made cards and mailed them to her instead of sending a gift. But this year they wanted to come up with a gift on their own. They wanted it to be something she would really treasure. Rebecca was now in seventh grade. She told Jake, a fourth grader, that they were old enough to take on this task for themselves.

Like many grandmothers, Nana already had whatever she needed. They did not want to give her another box of stationery or a houseplant. They wanted her to know that they had given lots of thought to the gift. Also, they wanted to pick something that she would always remember was from them. During their visit, they had found that Nana was a grandmother who did not stay at home and knit. She was involved in her community, and she shared many interests with her friends.

A gift for someone else should be something that the giver would like, Rebecca thought. But the things that they thought *they* would like did not fit their grandmother's life. "I don't think she'd really like a video game," Jake said. And Rebecca knew that her own tastes were quite different from her grandmother's. Rebecca had just gotten a new tennis racquet for her own birthday. It had been the perfect gift for her. She knew that it would not be for Nana, though. Nana did not play tennis.

Instead, they decided to brainstorm about Nana's interests. They would try to find something that went with what she liked to do.

Rebecca had learned from her English teacher about lotus flower diagrams. Her class had used this tool to think of ideas for writing topics. So she taught Jake how to make the diagram.

First, Rebecca took a large piece of brown wrapping paper and folded it in thirds lengthwise. Then she turned it and folded it in thirds sideways. She drew lines where the folds were, making a large chart (Figure 3.1). They already knew the topic to explore. It was Nana's interests. Rebecca wrote that in the center of the diagram.

She told Jake that they would first write the issue or challenge in the square in the middle of the diagram. Rebecca wrote "what Nana likes to do." They would brainstorm about Nana's interests. Then they would write ideas about that topic in the eight small squares around the center. Each of these had a letter of the alphabet in it, starting with *A* and ending with *H*. These can be put in any pattern you wish. Rebecca started with the bottom center and made a diamond, then filled in the others.

They came up with eight different interests that they decided were Nana's favorite activities. These were gardening, reading, writing letters, cooking, antiques, tandem bicycling, volunteering at church, and golf. Their lotus flower diagram began to look like Figure 3.2.

The next step, Rebecca said, was to put each of those eight ideas into its own square. Each one would then have eight new, related ideas. All

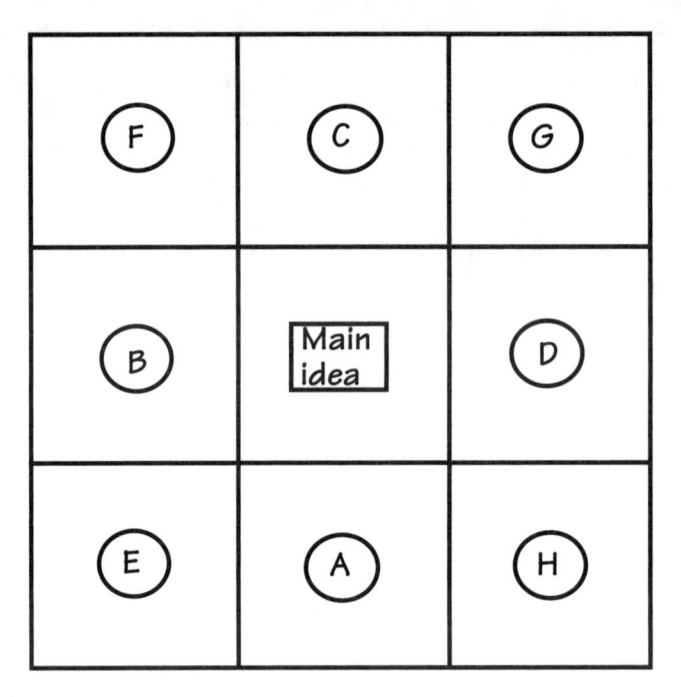

FIGURE 3.1 Blank lotus flower diagram

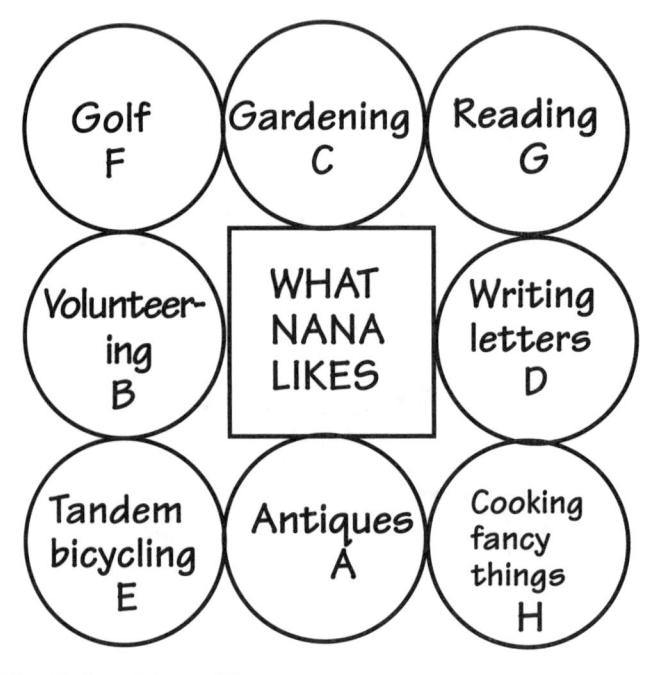

FIGURE 3.2 What Nana likes

the new lotus blossoms would be related to one of the original interests. The diagram, like the ancient lotus flower, would "open up." Depending on how far they wanted to go with their thinking, it would grow wider and wider and expand the possibilities. Jake was a little doubtful. "What if we get too many ideas?" he wondered. But Rebecca assured him. "Right now we have *no* ideas. So that would definitely be an improvement," she pointed out.

After they had come up with enough ideas, they reviewed Nana's interests. They decided that bicycling and golf were the ones they liked best. They made two lotus flower diagrams to get ideas about these (Figure 3.3). These diagrams were really extensions from the original squares labelled "tandem bicycling" and "golf."

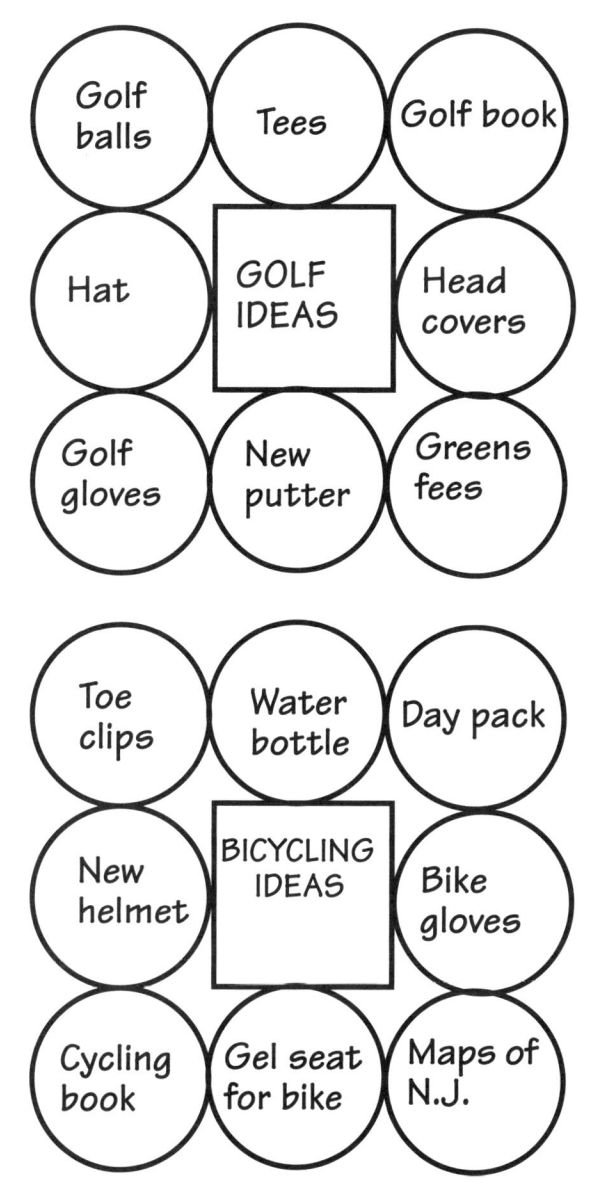

FIGURE 3.3 Golf and bicycling ideas

38 CHAPTER 3

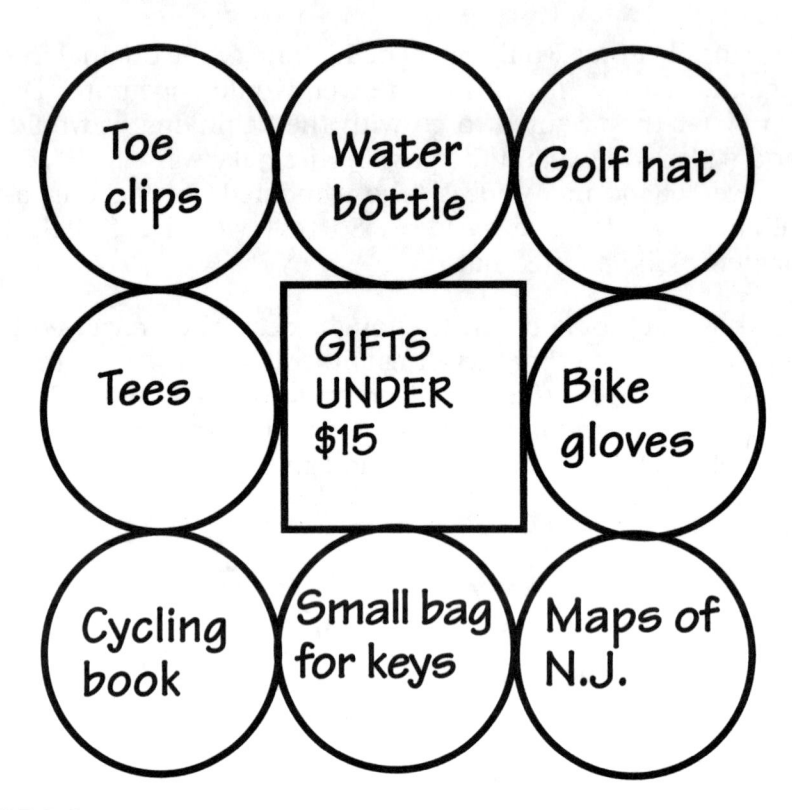

FIGURE 3.4 Gifts under $15

From here, the two needed to decide. Was cycling or golf a better gift idea? How much money did they have? It would be nice to buy Nana a new golf club, but they knew that was not possible. Rebecca and Jake put some limits on their gift. Then they decided that they wanted a bicycle-related gift. They used the lotus flower diagram again. This time, they wrote "Ideas under $15" in the center. With that limit, they thought of ideas for gifts that fit. They eliminated the golf club. They also crossed off the new gel seat for Nana's bike, but they expanded their list. The diagram looked like Figure 3.4.

Finally, they decided that Nana would like new bicycle gloves. She rode on her tandem bike with her friend from church almost every week. Rebecca and Jake decided to go to the bike store and see what they could find. They knew that they had other choices if they could not find a pair of gloves for less than $15. They felt confident about making their selection. They had not even argued about the gift!

Jake and Rebecca were able to find a gift for their grandmother that pleased her. It reflected her own interests and needs. Because they had given lots of thought to it, they were also able to find something that *they* liked as well. "Maybe that's what people mean when they say you should get a gift you'd pick for yourself," Rebecca decided.

LOTUS FLOWER DIAGRAMS **39**

SUGGESTIONS FOR USING THE LOTUS FLOWER DIAGRAM

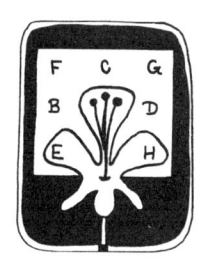

- Write your challenge or problem in the middle of the diagram.
- To help keep things straight, you may want to use different colors of construction paper in each square. Then, when you build additional lotus blossoms from the original, you can put each of those colors in the center of a new square.
- Think of enough ideas to fill the eight squares around the central issue. Then pick one of these to start a new lotus flower diagram.
- Remember that you are *opening up* your thinking about the issue you have selected. This is a tool that will help make your thinking more clear. You can let it *blossom* as widely as you wish.

OTHER TOOLS YOU MAY USE WITH LOTUS FLOWER DIAGRAMS

If you started with chapter 1, you have already learned two of these tools. You will learn about the others in later chapters. Don't be afraid to look ahead if you want to!

- Brainstorming, to come up with related ideas

- Affinity exercise, to group your ideas

- Check sheets, to collect data about specific ideas

- Fishbone diagrams, to identify root causes related to an issue

NAME: _____

CLASS: _____

DATE: _____

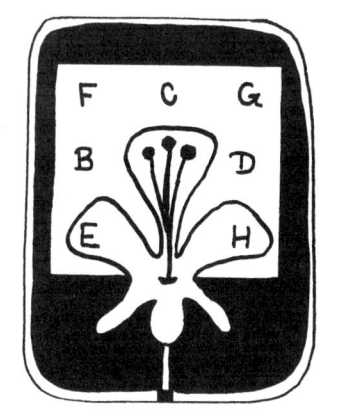

MY OWN THINKING TOOLS PAGE
LOTUS FLOWER DIAGRAMS

First, Some Practice

Before you make your own lotus flower diagram, practice thinking of themes or issues. A theme is an idea that connects other ideas together. An issue may be a problem or something you want to change. Some examples of themes are given below.

Look at the ideas listed below. Pick a theme you want to use for lotus flower thinking. You may want to use your own idea rather than using these. It might be best to select a topic that you can work on with another student or a small group of people.

Here are some ideas for you to think about:

1. Class projects related to slavery
2. Activities for a rainy day
3. Poem topics
4. Ways to say "thank you"
5. Celebrations for French Day
6. Articles for class newsletter
7. Places to hide in the classroom
8. Ways to make school more fun
9. How to earn money at home
10. Things to do with a pet
11. Ways to share our hobbies

If you use your own ideas instead of these, be sure to pick something that you really want to think about. After you choose an idea, write it in the middle box. Use the lotus flower diagram at the end of this chapter or make a copy of it on larger paper.

Put your first-round thinking in the circles around the middle box. Move these to new boxes. Then think of new ideas that are related. You may find that some of your ideas do not seem connected with the first one. This is a sign that your imagination is really blossoming. Who knows where it will lead?

Thinking of ideas is just the beginning of using the lotus flower diagram. When you move the ideas to their own boxes, you are coming up with new ideas. This can go on and on. You can take the lotus flower blossom as far out as you want. It is almost unlimited. Any time you want to open up and expand your thinking, this is a good tool to use.

Did you think of things that seemed *far out* from the original theme or issue? Which of the ideas are your favorites?

1. _____
2. _____
3. _____
4. _____

Now It's Your Turn...

With a partner or small group, write your own ideas for the middle box of a lotus flower diagram. Think of problems or challenges that you find at home, at school, on vacation, or in your play time. List them here.

1. _____
2. _____
3. _____
4. _____

You may not have enough space to write your ideas. Ask your teacher to enlarge the lotus flower diagram at the end of this chapter for you to use. You can make your own by drawing the lines and shapes on a large sheet of paper or on the blackboard in your classroom. Remember how Rebecca folded a large sheet of paper before drawing lines on it? How far can you make your lotus flower diagram go? Whenever it grows, your thinking is also growing.

HOME CONNECTION

Lotus flower diagrams help to capture creative ideas. These may be for solving problems or simply stretching possibilities. Try using this tool with your family. Here are some ideas to start with. Write one of them in the center box, and expand from there.

1. Our family vacation
2. Gift ideas (for anyone)
3. Where to store things in the house
4. Weekend plans
5. A pet for the family
6. Chores that must be done
7. Earning money for camp
8. Places to do homework
9. Ways to celebrate a birthday
10. Nice things to do for neighbors

NAME: _____

CLASS: _____

DATE: _____

LOTUS FLOWER DIAGRAM TEMPLATE

This is a blank square to begin your lotus flower diagram. Remember to put an idea in the center of each square, starting with the middle. Then write related ideas around it. The small lotus flower diagram here shows where to write your ideas.

F	C	G
B	Main idea	D
E	A	H

45

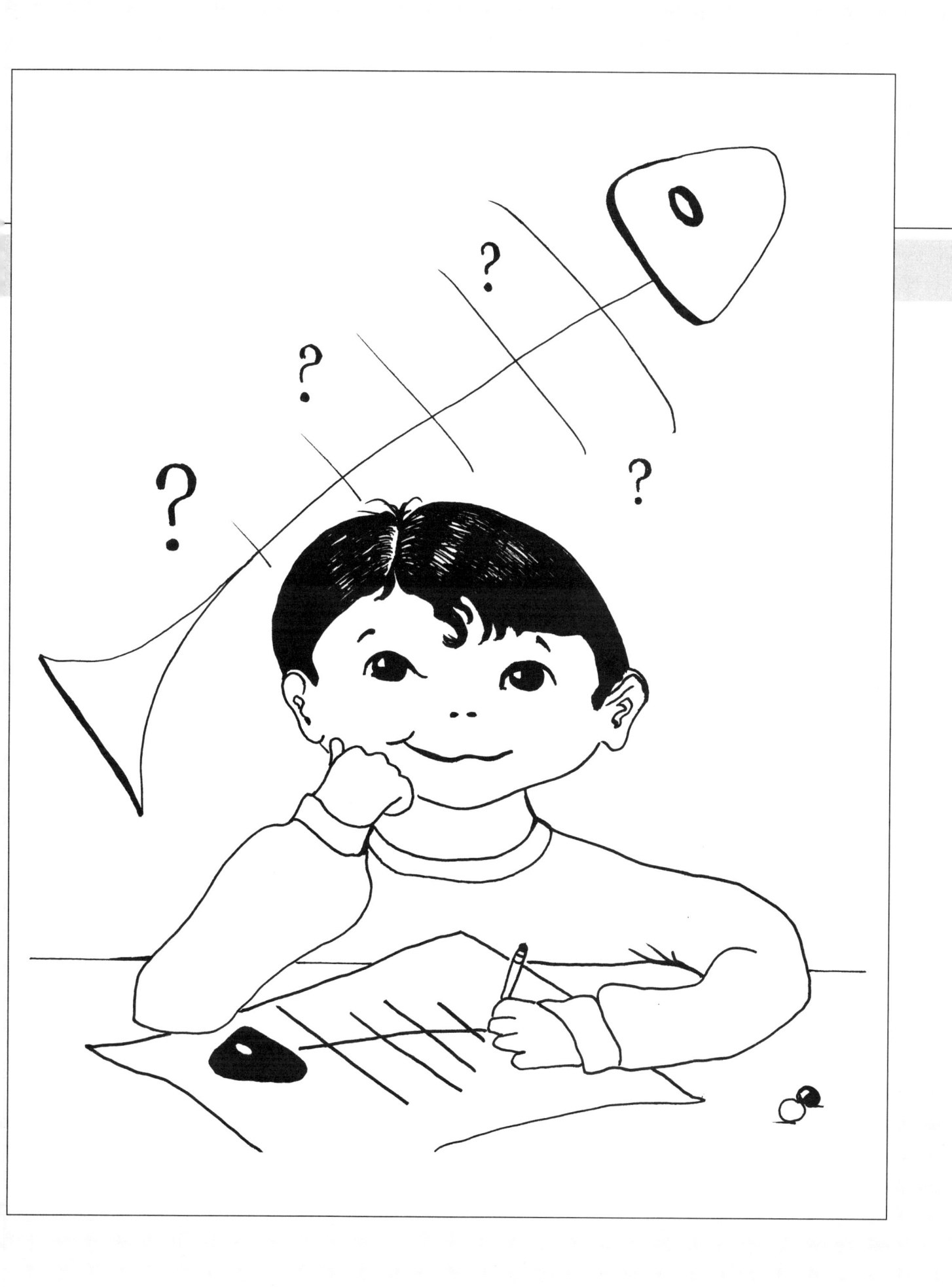

SECTION II

TOOLS FOR MAKING CONNECTIONS

CHAPTER 4

FISHBONE DIAGRAMS
Catching the Cause

Tommy liked to get up early on weekends and have breakfast with his father. His dad was also an early riser. The two of them would take their dog Molly for a walk. When they got back, they would make breakfast for the rest of the family.

When Tommy was younger, his dad had always done the cooking. As Tommy got older, he began to help out. First, he would pour juice and set the table. Later he was actually preparing food. "Pretty soon, I can just read the paper and drink my coffee and you'll be making the whole breakfast," his dad said. So far, Tommy had learned to make French toast.

Tommy's father emphasized that making French toast, like other things that one does, is a *process*. That is, it involves a series of steps that all lead to its completion. Later, you will see how he used a flowchart (chapter 7) to organize the steps in the process of making French toast.

The trouble was that Tommy's French toast did not always turn out the same way. Sometimes it was crisp and almost burned. Once, he had had to scrape it out of the pan when it stuck. Most of the time, however, it was still soft and wet on the inside, and not very brown on the outside. His family never complained. When he sat down to eat with them, though, he was aware of the different results on the big platter. He looked at the beautiful color photo of French toast that appeared next to the recipe in the cookbook. Tommy wondered why his French toast never looked quite like that.

It was discouraging to go through what seemed like the same steps each time, and then not be able to tell how his French toast would turn out. The question was *why*.

Tommy decided to use a *fishbone diagram* that he had learned about at school. The tool is called a fishbone diagram because it looks like the skeleton of a fish. The purpose of the fishbone diagram, his teacher said, is to get to the *main causes* for something. This can be something either good or bad. A fishbone diagram can help to figure out why a process works well, like the class play. It could also help to explain outcomes like grades. It is a way to look at a process.

His class had practiced using this tool, also called a *cause-and-effect diagram,* to review reasons for the success of their class play. When they had performed it for their parents, the production had no problems at all. Everyone had remembered lines and cues, the audience applauded a lot, and the costumes and props had been exactly right. The process of performing the play had been successful.

To analyze the reasons for this success, Tommy's class had drawn the *bones* of the fishbone diagram on the board in their classroom. On the right side, they wrote "Successful play." They divided the major bones of the diagram to show four different kinds of reasons. These were "people," "materials," "techniques," and "environment." Mrs. Haynes, their

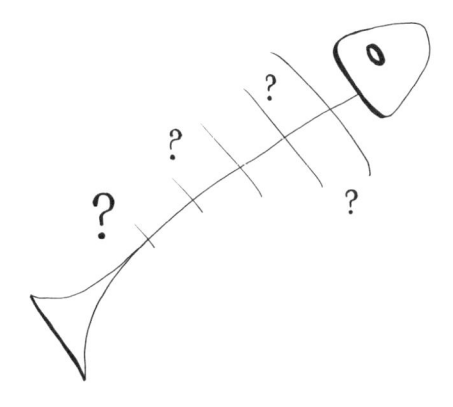

50 CHAPTER 4

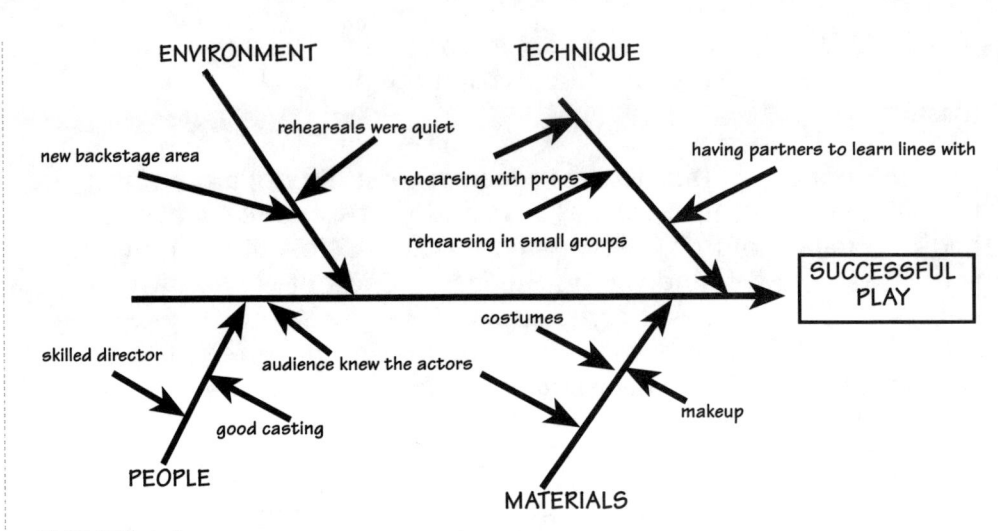

FIGURE 4.1 Causes for successful play

teacher, helped them to select these groups, which seemed to fit the process they were describing.

The class brainstormed all the possible contributions to the success of the play. They wrote these on the major bones of their diagram. Each major area had different items under it. Their finished fishbone diagram appears in Figure 4.1.

Tommy figured that because making French toast is a process, a fishbone diagram would work as well on this as on any other process, including producing and performing the play. So he made the same kind of outline shape for his French toast question. Instead of looking for main causes for its success, however, he was looking for reasons that it was not so good.

At first, Tommy wrote down the reasons he could think of himself. Then he decided he should bring his family into the discussion as well. One morning he cleared the breakfast dishes from the table. Then he brought his diagram and taped it to the wall in the kitchen. "Why do you think my French toast isn't always good?" he asked, explaining how to use the chart.

Sarah, his sister, was a good cook, although she did not like to make breakfast, and she had never made French toast. "Maybe your skillet isn't hot enough," she offered, to get the ideas started. At first, Tommy wanted to argue with her. After all, it was his French toast, and he had tried his best. Then he remembered that he really wanted to make it better, after all. He needed to listen to everyone, even those who had never made French toast. "You never know where a good idea will come from," Mrs. Haynes had said to his class. He wrote Sarah's idea on the diagram.

Everyone offered ideas, and Tommy wrote them on his chart where they seemed to fit. Figure 4.2 shows what it looked like after everyone had suggested ideas for causes.

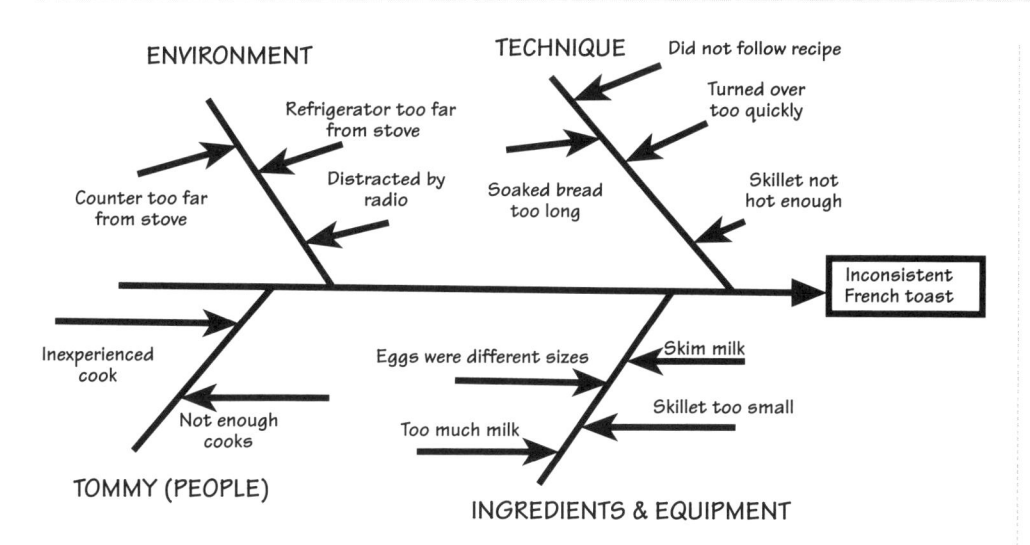

FIGURE 4.2 French toast fishbone diagram

Tommy looked at the diagram. He saw lots of reasons that his French toast might not have been as good as he wanted it to be. He wanted to test some of the causes to find out if they were contributing to the outcome. That way, he could eliminate many of those listed. After all, brainstorming for the fishbone diagram was meant to help everyone think about all the possible causes. His family had been creative in their suggestions. Since he had been making French toast for several weeks, he was able to focus on what he thought was the most likely reason, or the *main cause*. This is sometimes called the *root cause*.

Fishbone diagrams help to get to the bottom of things. They solve the mystery of *why?*

To understand the problem further, Tommy wrote what he thought was the main cause on a blank diagram. His family's

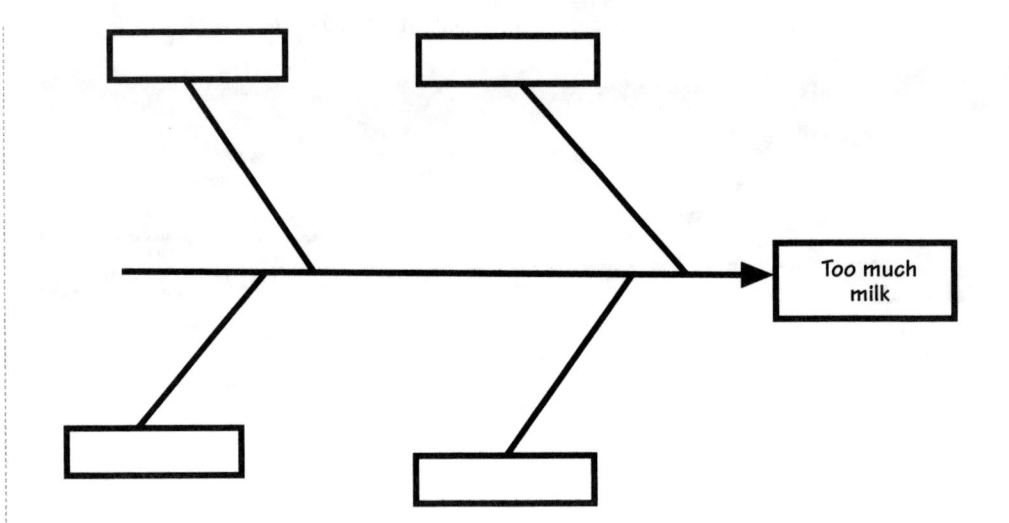

FIGURE 4.3 Too much milk: Fishbone diagram

comments helped him to gradually eliminate some of the causes as less important. Finally, he circled "too much milk" and wrote this on a on a new fishbone diagram (Figure 4.3). He asked for reasons that this might be happening.

In this round of brainstorming, many new ideas were given:

> reading the recipe wrong
> not measuring correctly
> using skim milk
> measuring cup is incorrect
> adding milk twice
> doubling milk without doubling eggs in recipe
> recipe is wrong
> measuring cup has no marks

By this time, Tommy knew what the problem was. He remembered that he had not been measuring carefully. He had been simply splashing milk into the egg mixture from the carton. After all, it was such a small amount of milk. He thought it probably would not make much difference.

Tommy changed his method of measuring and pouring the milk, and the next morning his family enjoyed perfect French toast from chef Tommy's kitchen.

No doubt Tommy could have figured this out for himself without the fishbone diagram. He might have tried correcting everything that might have gone wrong when he made French toast. He would have probably figured it out eventually. By thinking through the problem and looking at it in this step-by-step way, Tommy was fairly sure what the problem was before he tried the recipe again. If he had not done it this way, he might have wasted lots of ingredients before discovering the cause of the problem. And his family would have had lots of bad French toast in the meantime.

Sometimes when people try to solve problems, they change several things at once. They are eager to fix what is wrong. If it improves, they may not even know which factor made the difference. By using the fishbone diagram, the problem will be addressed in a systematic, step-by-step way. This helps to think through what needs to be done.

SUGGESTIONS FOR USING FISHBONE DIAGRAMS:

- As with any brainstorming, there should be no judgment about ideas when people say them. The point is to create as many causes as possible.
- Everyone will have an opinion about what causes a problem. Organizing these ideas improves the chance that good ideas can be tested.
- Label the main *bones* of the fishbone in ways that are best for your problem or event.
- You can use the fishbone diagram not only to get to the root of a problem, but to help with planning. Remember how Tommy's class analyzed their successful play. This helped them plan their next production.

OTHER TOOLS YOU MAY USE WITH FISHBONE DIAGRAMS

- Brainstorming, to come up with lots of ideas, as Tommy did

- Check sheets, to collect data about a theory or idea

- Line graphs, to see patterns and trends

NAME: _____

CLASS: _____

DATE: _____

MY OWN THINKING TOOLS PAGE
CAUSE-AND-EFFECT (FISHBONE) DIAGRAM

First, Some Practice

Suppose that you and a friend planned a 20-mile bicycle ride on a bike trail near your home. You were not able to finish the ride. Here is a list of possible reasons that the ride was not finished. First, brainstorm and record any other causes that you can think of, and add them to the list. Look at the list and decide on categories for each of the *bones* on the fishbone diagram that appears below. Write these in the boxes at the ends of the bones. Then write all the possible causes on the fishbone diagram.

flat tire	friend forgets lunch
chain falls off	wrong tires for rough terrain
brake cable breaks	handlebars become loose
not enough water	thunderstorm threatens
starts to rain	gets too dark
friend is injured	you decide to stop at baseball game
trail is closed	too hot and sunny

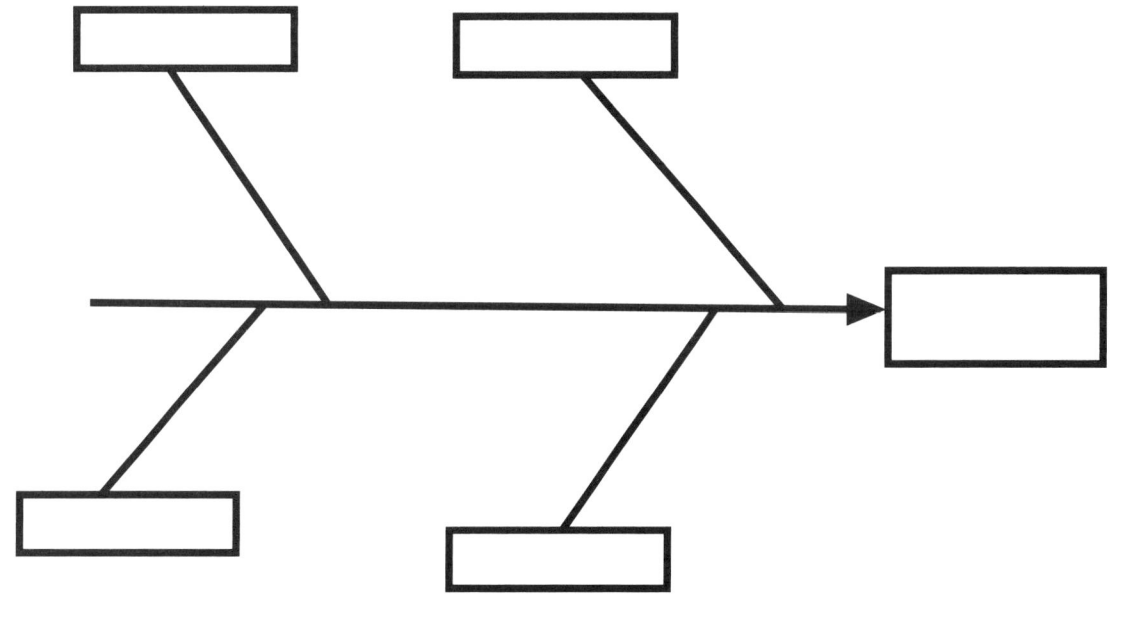

55

By placing these ideas on the fishbone diagram, you can focus on the main cause for a situation. Of course you are only imagining this trip, rather than actually thinking about a trip that you have taken with your friend. For this reason, you have no way to determine which of the items is really the main cause. This is a made-up example to help you write the causes on the fishbone.

To help make the trip go smoothly, you might imagine it before you actually go. How would this fishbone diagram help you plan for the trip? How could it help prevent some of the problems that might occur? Talk about this with a classmate, and write down ways that some of the causes might have been prevented.

1. _____
2. _____
3. _____
4. _____
5. _____

Now It's Your Turn...

Now think of a problem that you would like to solve. It might be something you want to improve or change. It may be related to one of the following:

- School (not paying attention in class, forgetting your homework, doing the wrong assignment, not following directions, being late to school, doing poorly on tests, missing school, taking too long to do work, losing papers, etc.)
- Home (not keeping your room clean, fighting with your brother, not getting enough allowance, forgetting to do chores, doing what you have promised, staying up too late, not eating at meals, not writing letters to grandparents, etc.)
- Hobbies (slump in batting average, spending too much on CDs, not enough money for tennis lessons, skateboard keeps breaking, overdue books at the library, not enough time to play, never getting to see newest movies, etc.)

Use a fishbone diagram to get to the mystery of *why?* for the problem you have selected. First, label the major bones with the names of categories that make sense to you. These are meant to help you think, so be sure they are clear.

With one or more partners, brainstorm possible causes for your problem. Even though your partners are not directly involved in it, they will be able to give you ideas. They can see what *might* be causing the problem, from different perspectives. Your partners may be classmates, family members, or others who have an interest in helping you improve.

First, make a list of the ideas, then record them on a fishbone diagram. You will find one at the end of this chapter. Circle what you think is the main cause for the problem. For example, if you are having trouble finishing your homework, a main cause might be that you begin your assignments too late in the evening and you become too tired to finish.

Next, create a second fishbone diagram, with the main cause from the first diagram as the *head* of the fishbone diagram. Maybe you wrote "going to bed too late," as a reason for not finishing your homework. Put "going to bed too late" at the head of a new fishbone. Label the main bones for that diagram, and again, brainstorm with your partners the things that may be creating the main cause.

What have you learned by making a fishbone diagram relating to this particular problem?

_____
_____
_____

What are some steps you can take to test your theory about the main cause(s) for the problem?

_____
_____
_____
_____
_____

For the future, list other ways that you might use the fishbone diagram to solve a problem or improve a situation.

_____
_____

A fishbone diagram is meant not only to solve problems, but to analyze success as well. Select something that has worked well for you, as Tommy's class did with the school play. Brainstorm some of the reasons for your success, and record these on a fishbone diagram. Some ideas about processes that have had positive outcomes:

1. Remembering to feed your dog or cat
2. Keeping your room neat
3. Enjoying art class

4. Finishing requirements for a merit badge in Scouting
5. Being selected for student council
6. Your own idea: _____

HOME CONNECTION

At home, there are always many mysteries to be solved. Solving the mystery of *why?* is sometimes the hardest. Here are some questions to get you started with fishbone diagrams at home. Brainstorm with your family to try to get to main causes. Think of some things you do at home for which you would like to understand the main cause.

1. Why do chores sometimes not get done?
2. Why do we need a curfew when we go to our friends' homes?
3. Why does the dog bark to go out and then want right back in?
4. Why was our vacation so much fun?
5. Why is Grandma so lonely?
6. Why is dinner always served at the same time each evening?

NAME: _____

CLASS: _____

DATE: _____

FISHBONE DIAGRAM TEMPLATE

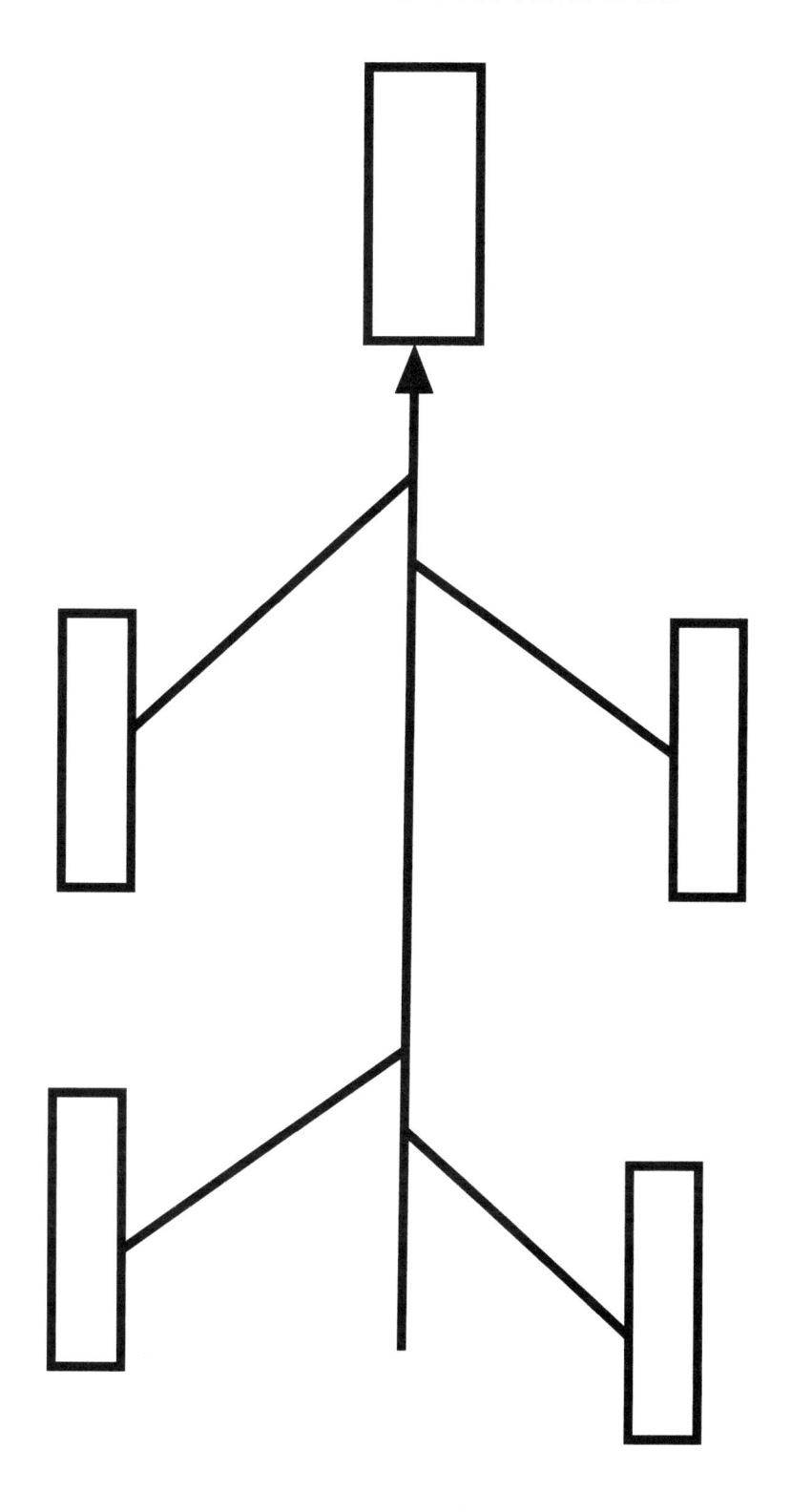

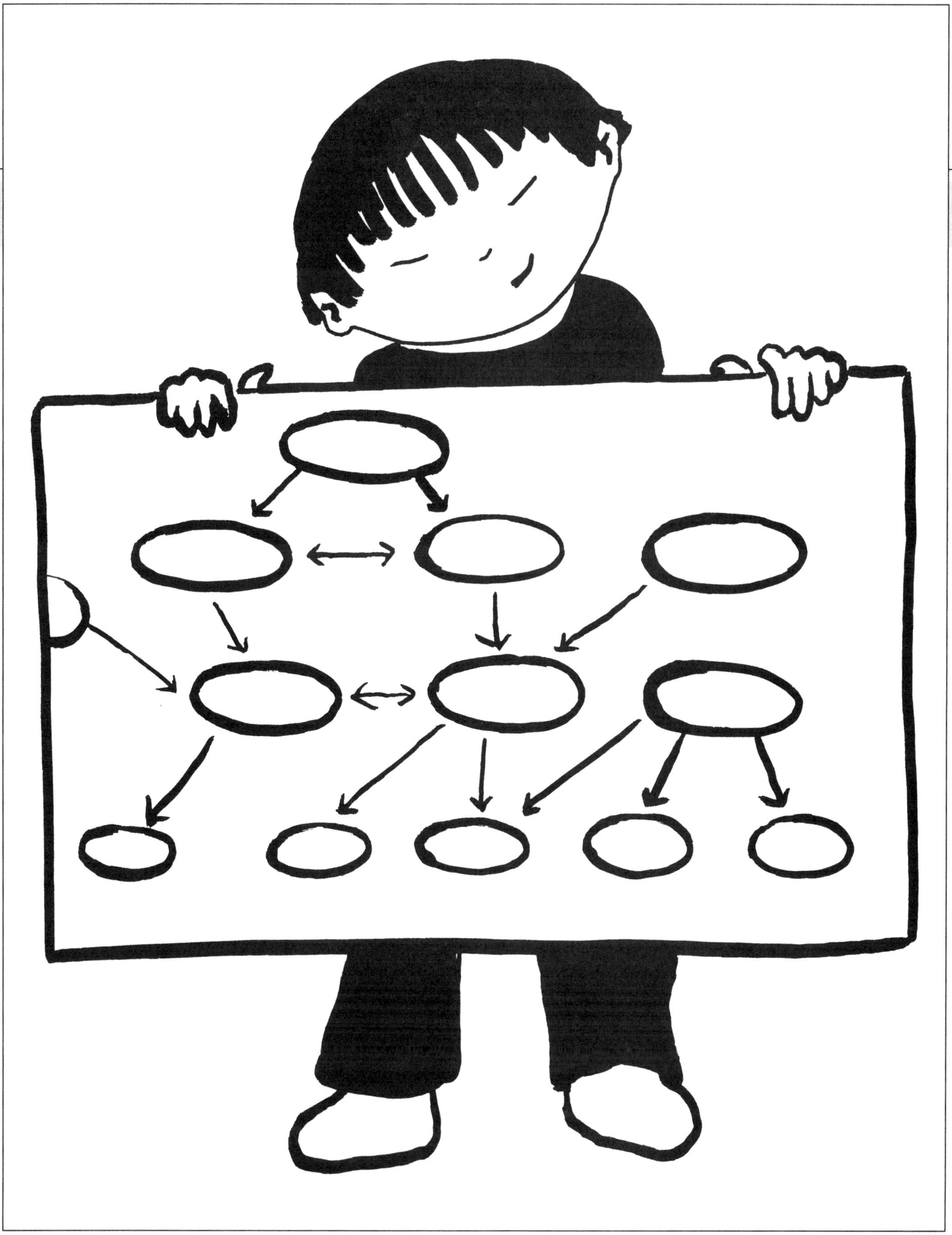

CHAPTER 5

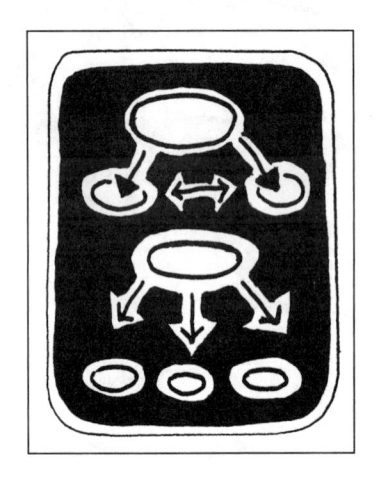

RELATIONS DIAGRAMS
Figuring Out the Connections

In the hallway near Michael's bedroom was a large photograph of lots of people. Someone had taken the picture at the Lee family reunion several years before. Michael had never met most of these people. Sometimes he would look at the picture and try to figure out who everyone was. Often he would give up. There were more than 40 people of all ages. Figuring out who belonged to which family was impossible.

Michael's father had a book that his own father had given to him. It had the names of 20 generations of Lees, his father said. The names were all written in Korean, in people's own handwriting. No dates were given, but Michael's father believed it went back more than 400 years. Michael had never seen the book. His father kept it locked in a safe place at the bank. But he had seen pictures of some of the pages. He remembered how old and cracked the pages looked, and how tiny the

Korean characters had seemed to him. Michael could not read Korean. His parents spoke the language, but he had not learned more than a few words.

One day Michael's mother announced that another family reunion was planned. Everyone in the Lee family was going to a dude ranch in Colorado for the reunion. It would be the following summer. She was in charge of getting T-shirts for everyone that said "I'm a Lee." The younger children would have shirts that said "I'm a Little Lee." Michael already decided he would not wear one of those. She would have to write to everyone to find their sizes and then order the shirts. Most of the family lived in California, where Michael's grandparents had first immigrated from Korea. Others lived in Chicago, Boston, and Cleveland.

For the reunion, they decided that Colorado would be a good meeting place. None of them had ever been to a dude ranch. Michael had never ridden a horse. His father said he had not either. "This will be a new experience," his mother said enthusiastically. It was her idea.

Michael was worried more about faces than about the T-shirts or the horses. He really wanted to figure out who was related to whom. Several of the young people in the picture seemed to be close to his own age. If he knew who they were, it would help him get to know them at the reunion.

When he asked his mother to tell him about someone in the picture, it was quite confusing. "That's Paul. He is one of the twins. His mother, Miyung, is married to my cousin Sang. Sang was married before, but his first wife, Mai, died. They had two little girls, Annie and Amy. Sang and Miyung are the girls' parents now."

Michael tried to remember all the names and the ways that the people in the picture were connected. He was really confused. Finally his older brother, Bennie, said he'd help him figure out a system for knowing who the adults in the picture were, and which children belonged to each adult. They could also figure out who was related and who was not.

Bennie got a big sheet of paper. He and Michael took the photograph off the wall and put it on the table so they could look at it while they made their diagram of all the relationships in the picture.

64 CHAPTER 5

"You don't have to remember the names of the people who died, like Mai," said Bennie. "That just makes it too confusing. Also, people who are married will have one box together. We'll put dotted lines between their names on the chart." But first, he drew a circle and put a name in it. "That's Paul." Then he drew others for Paul's parents, Sang and Miyung, and his grandparents, Jennie and Tony. He drew arrows from the parents' circles to Paul's, and from the grandparents' circles to Paul's mother's name. The first sketch looked like Figure 5.1 at this point.

Bennie transferred this draft information to a relations chart. He drew a line with arrows on both ends from Allison to Paul, to show that they were members of the same family. That is, they had the same parents. "Now Sang's parents are Mother's aunt and uncle, Jennie and Tony," Bennie explained. He drew a box with a dotted line for them, and then drew arrows to Sang's name from theirs.

The next children that Bennie picked were Annie and Amy, and their lines were similar to Paul and Allison's. "Let's do us now," Michael said.

"Okay. We'll write `Michael' and `Bennie,' and put boxes around them. We both have Henry and Josephine for parents. Our mother, Josephine, is the daughter of Robin and Chang-Rae." Bennie drew an arrow from these two to Josephine. Then he put a double arrow between the two boys' names. Since Tony is the brother of Robin, he put a double arrow between those names as well. They are children of the same parents.

"The others are a little trickier," Bennie said. "Let's take Grandfather." Grandfather was really their great-grandfather, who was quite old but had come to the last reunion. He is the father of Tony, and also the father of Robin. Bennie put a double arrow between those two names. Grandfather also had two other children, Rose and Caroline, who now

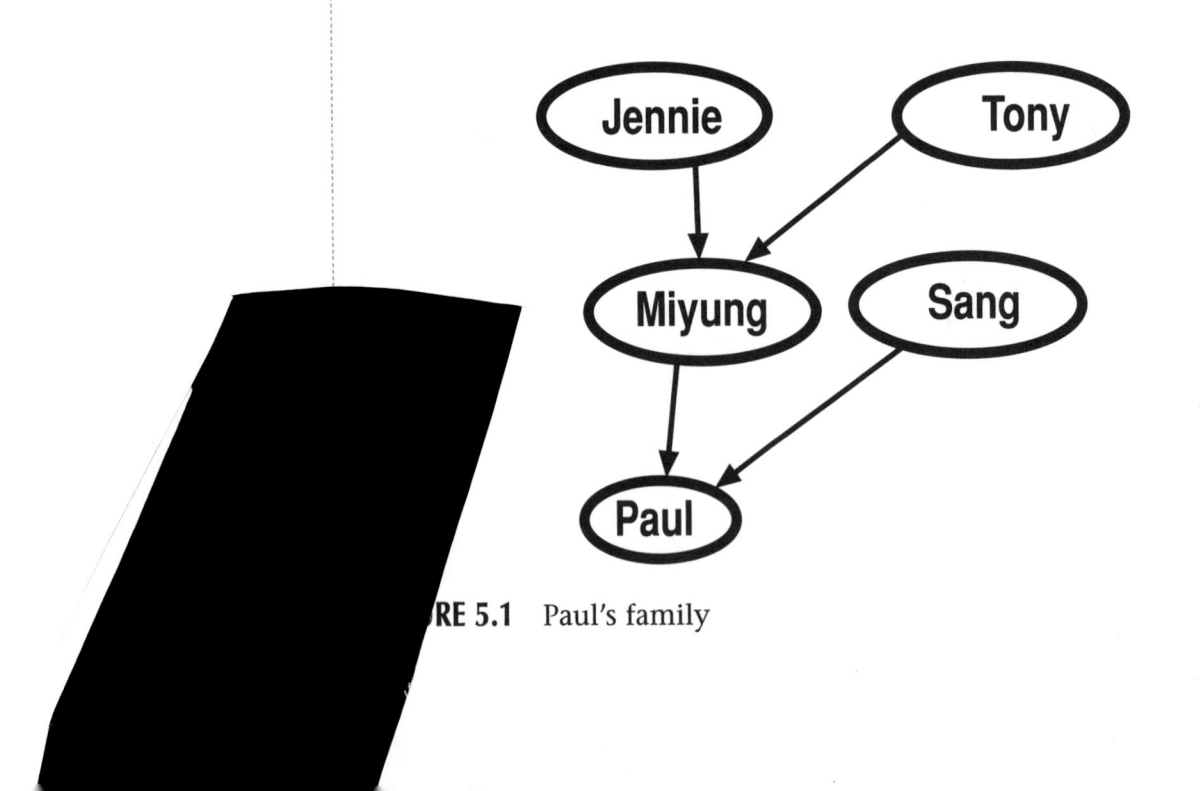

FIGURE 5.1 Paul's family

had children of their own. Bennie wrote their names down and showed their relationships to the others with single and double arrows. The chart looked like Figure 5.2.

There were other cousins who were related in some way, and Bennie drew diagrams for all the people he knew about. They had to ask their mother about some of the names. She thought that Bennie had done a great job of remembering so many names and the ways that they were related. After several days, the diagram was growing even more. "It's not finished, but that gives us a good start," Bennie said. "Bring on the dude ranch and 'I'm a Lee' T-shirts!"

Bennie was drawing a chart of relationships among family members. His chart showed the parent-child and brother-sister relationships in the Lee family.

The thinking tool that is known as a *relations diagram* shows relationships, too. It helps to sort out cause-and-effect relationships, or what causes what, rather than who is related to whom. Bennie and Michael had a purpose in drawing their diagram. They wanted to see who was related. In fact, Michael Lee wanted an answer to the question, "Who in the world is Paul?"

They wanted to know which names were parents and children, and which ones were brothers and sisters. So they had different kinds of arrows. The single arrows showed parent-child relationships, and the double arrows showed brother-sister relationships. To show these same family relationships, they might have considered a *family tree* diagram. A family tree shows parents and their children, and lines are used to connect the relationships. A family tree is a kind of relations diagram. Bennie thought a less structured drawing was more helpful to teach Michael about people in the family.

A relations diagram that is used to sort out causes is similar to Bennie's chart. Each idea or factor is put in a box. Then arrows show what

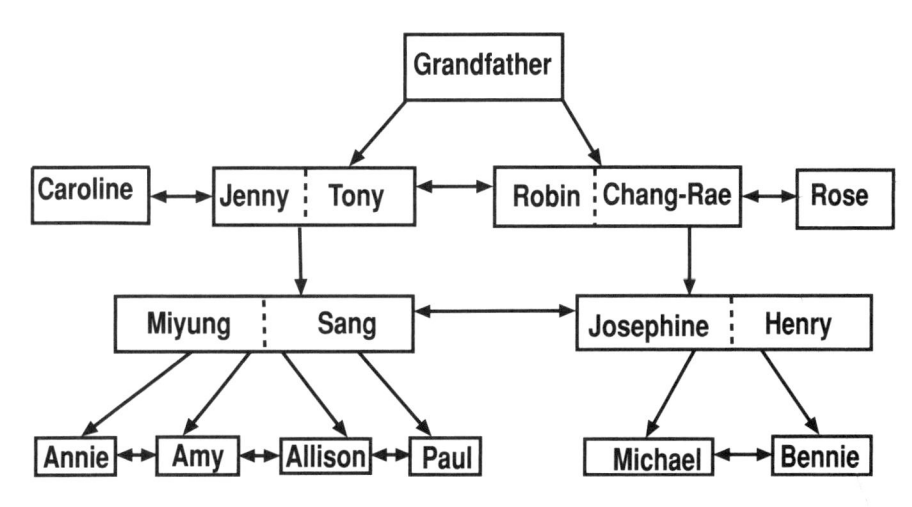

FIGURE 5.2 Lee family

causes what. As you saw in chapter 4, fishbone diagrams are another way to show causes. In the fishbone diagram, different parts of a problem contribute as causes. The parts can be "people," "equipment," "methods," or other aspects that you choose. Different aspects may not seem to be related. They are separate causes for the same outcome. With a relations diagram, it is easier to see how different aspects of an issue are related. In Bennie's relations diagram, one might think of the parents as *causes* for the children. The parents' relationships to their own parents becomes clearer in the diagram. In addition, the relationships of others who are related but not as parents is easier to understand.

To apply the relations diagram to an issue, let's take a common playground problem. The primary grades have just gotten a new piece of equipment for their playground. It is an immense wood pirate ship, with an upper deck, and rings and bars to climb to the top. It has a ladder and a small cabin where children can play.

Everyone loves the pirate ship, including the older children in the school. Grades 4 and 5 have a separate area of the playground, and grades 6–8 have an area of their own as well. When the younger children come out to play, they find that their pirate ship is being used by the older students. It makes them unhappy. They are afraid to say anything to the older students, but they have complained to their teachers.

Teachers often tell the older children to get off the pirate ship and go back to their own areas. These adults are watching the entire primary playground, however, so they cannot always see the older children. Besides, they would like the children to solve the problem, rather than being police officers all the time. The teachers want to help students understand the causes of the problem in order to find the best solution. They decide to form a team to look at the situation. On the team are two teachers, three children from primary grades 1–3, and one each from fourth grade through eighth grade.

Forming a team to look at causes takes away the blame for something. The teachers could have just told the older kids to go away, or punished them for using the pirate ship. They decided instead that it was important to look at the reasons for the problem. A relations diagram helped.

The group wrote "Older students using the primary playground equipment." Then they brainstormed about all the issues that are related to this, and all the aspects of the problem that they could think of. Figure 5.3 reflects their thinking.

Next, they looked at each issue. They asked how it related to the other issues. When an issue seemed to influence another issue, they drew an arrow from it. The arrow went to another box that was related. For example, the amount of time each group had for recess seemed to be influenced by the location of the primary area. Location was also influenced by the fact that older children had recess earlier. Recess times

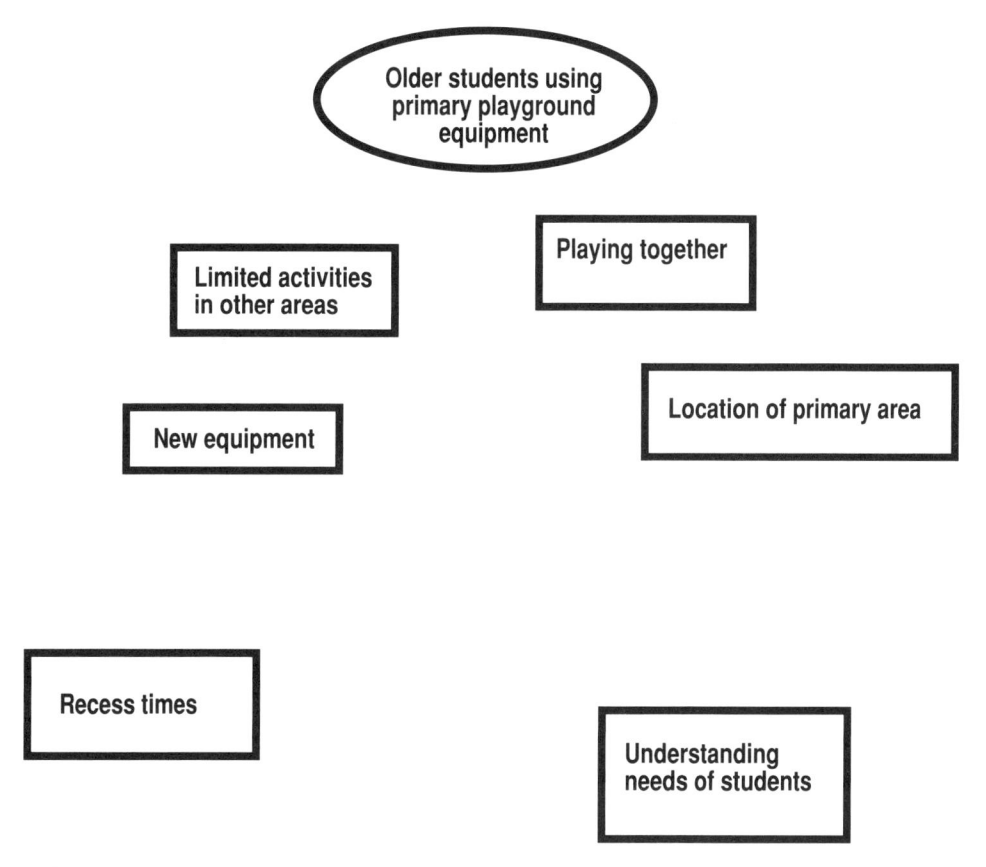

FIGURE 5.3 Issues related to playground use

were short, so the older children went to the primary area first because it was closer.

The issue of playing together also seems to influence the times of recess. That is, teachers did not want older and younger children playing together, but they wanted them to at least see each other. Therefore, they tried to schedule overlapping playground times, but not too much time. They were afraid that older students might hurt the younger children (or the other way around).

The team analyzed the issues, and drew arrows to show the influences among them. Then they looked at the diagram (Figure 5.4). They counted the number of arrows in and the numbers of arrows out of each box. The box with the greatest number of arrows out is the issue that has the greatest influence on the others. The one with the greatest number of arrows in is the one that is affected most by other areas.

The team sees that the box with the greatest number of arrows out is "understanding needs of students." The one with the greatest number of arrows in is "recess times." They decided that "understanding needs of students" was important. It shows that older children as well

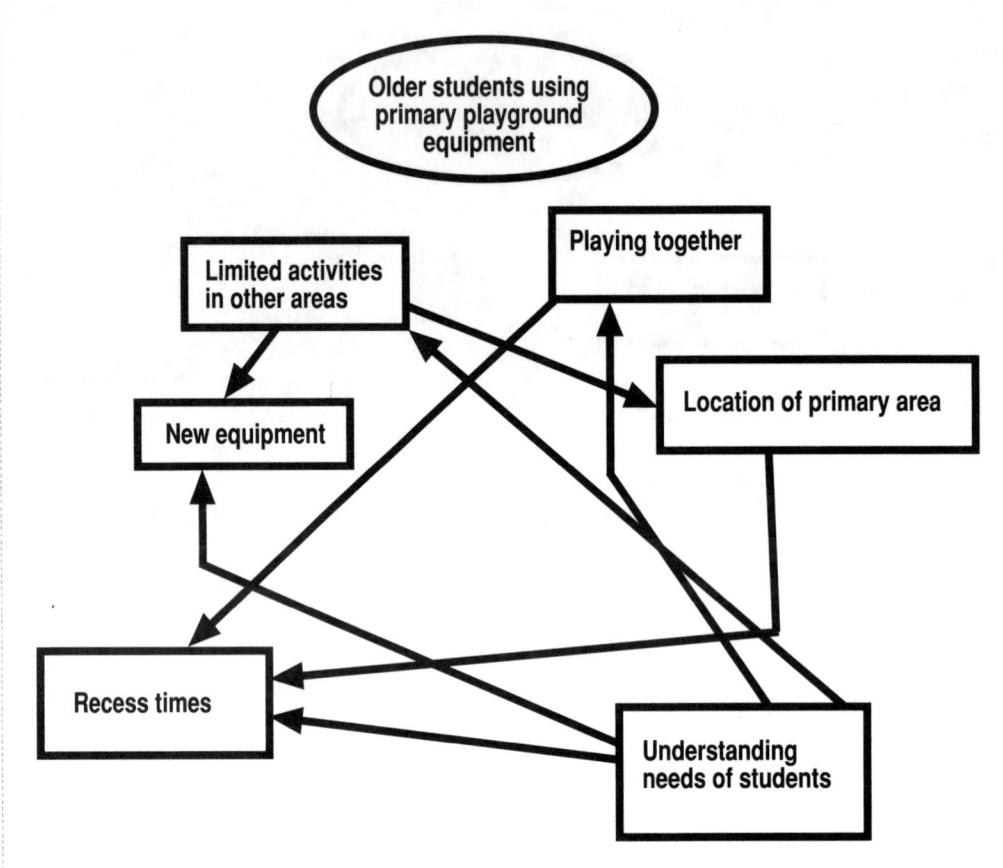

FIGURE 5.4 Issues and their relationships

as younger children need time to play. They also need playground equipment that they like.

The relations diagram shows relationships among parts of a problem. It also points the way for further study. The team may want to explore the ways that different student needs affect the playground issue. They will also want to look at recess itself for possible solutions to the problem. A relations diagram is useful when issues are complex or when they seem to be unrelated.

SUGGESTIONS FOR USING RELATIONS DIAGRAMS

- Remember that relations diagrams are useful in looking at complex issues.
- A relations diagram is not something that can be done quickly. Often, it takes several meetings to come up with all the related issues.
- The issues in a relations diagram can change, and the relations diagram itself can change. It is a *dynamic* tool; that is, it is never really finished, but changes often.

- After one of the issues has been addressed further, another relations diagram can be made to see if other major issues can be identified.

OTHER TOOLS YOU MAY USE WITH RELATIONS DIAGRAMS

- Brainstorming, to develop ideas about issues

- Flowchart, to show a process that contributes to a problem or issue

- Check sheet, to gather data about a particular issue

- Pareto chart, to show most frequent occurrences of a particular cause

NAME: _____

CLASS: _____

DATE: _____

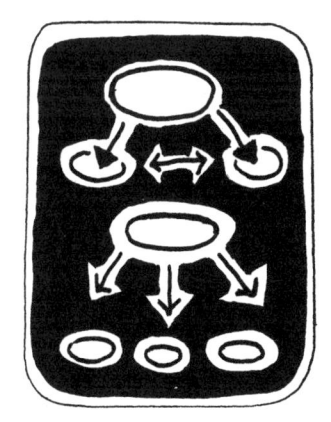

MY OWN THINKING TOOLS PAGE
RELATIONS DIAGRAMS

First, Some Practice

As a class or in a small group, select one of the problems or issues listed below. Write this in the center of a relations diagram. You may use the blank form that appears on the last page of this chapter. You can also draw your own on a big sheet of paper. If you choose to use the one that is provided, ask your teacher to make two copies of the page for you. Write your issues as a list first. After you are finished, write the issues in the squares on the relations diagram. Add more squares if you need them. Cut out the squares on one copy and arrange them on a table so you can move them around to show relationships. Then write them on the uncut copy and draw the arrows that you need.

After you have chosen an issue and written it on your diagram, think of all the issues that are related to it. Be as creative as you can. Think of reasons that the problem exists. Think also about issues that influence it. Include all of these in your diagram.

Some topics from which to choose:

1. Lines are too long for lunch
2. Not enough time in the library
3. Things being taken from desks or lockers
4. Clocks in the school show different times
5. Litter on the playground
6. Understanding school rules
7. Knowing about tornado and fire drills
8. Becoming acquainted with other students in the school
9. Knowing who the teachers are in the school
10. Welcoming students who are new to the school or class
11. Making visitors feel welcome in our classroom
12. Other (you think of one)

After you have brainstormed about related issues and written them on your diagram, discuss each one of these carefully. Think about how each one influences one or more of the other issues. If you have cut out the squares, arrange them so you can see their relationships. Draw your arrows to show these relationships. Keep going until you have talked about all the issues. If anyone thinks of a new issue or influence, include that one too.

Count all the arrows, both in and out. Which of the issues seems to be the greatest cause or influence on the others? Which one seems to be the greatest effect? Write these in the spaces below:

Greatest cause:_____

Major effect: _____

Now It's Your Turn...

A relations diagram, like brainstorming, is a group exercise. It helps everyone in a group to understand complex issues. Like the fishbone diagram, it is a thinking tool that helps sort out causes and relationships. Form a small group to practice a little further with this tool. You can even do the following exercise by yourself. Remember, though, that the relations diagram is most useful for larger groups or more complex problems.

In your group, pick something that you are studying in your class or something that you have already learned. For example, you may be studying different states or regions of the United States. Use your book if you need to, in order to remember different concepts that are related.

Here's an example of a relations diagram that addresses a school topic. Think of all the factors that are related to the exploration of the West. Some of the issues include:

Lewis and Clark's exploration

The role of different presidents of the U.S.

Native peoples

Crops and resources

Wildlife

Transportation

Communication

Family life

The writings of explorers

List other issues that might be related to the central topic here:

_____   _____   _____

_____   _____   _____

_____   _____   _____

Make a relations diagram that shows these and other issues, and draw the arrows to indicate how they influenced one another. Does this help to show how complex the issue of exploration and settlement really is?

Try this on your own, with a topic you may be studying or one in which you have a special interest. Some other ideas for you to do with your group, explore the influences or issues related to the following:

1. The clothes that we wear
2. Daylight savings time
3. Political elections
4. Our water supply
5. Planting trees
6. A famous person
7. Race or gender stereotypes
8. Staying healthy

HOME CONNECTION

You may want to brainstorm with your family members to list issues that need their attention. Teach family members about relations diagrams and how this tool helps to sort out different issues and shows how they are related to each other. Here are some ideas for you try at home:

1. Budgeting family resources (time, money, use of television or computer)
2. Determining how tasks are done in the family
3. Fairness issues
4. Making decisions as a family
5. How our family treats guests
6. Transportation issues
7. Community service opportunities for our family
8. Dealing with grandparents
9. Religious practices in our family
10. How we learn from each other

NAME: _____

CLASS: _____

DATE: _____

RELATIONS DIAGRAM TEMPLATE

Topic or issue: _____

Related issues: Write these in the squares that are provided, then draw arrows to show relationships among them. You can also use a giant sheet of paper to write your issues, so you will have more room for making connections among them.

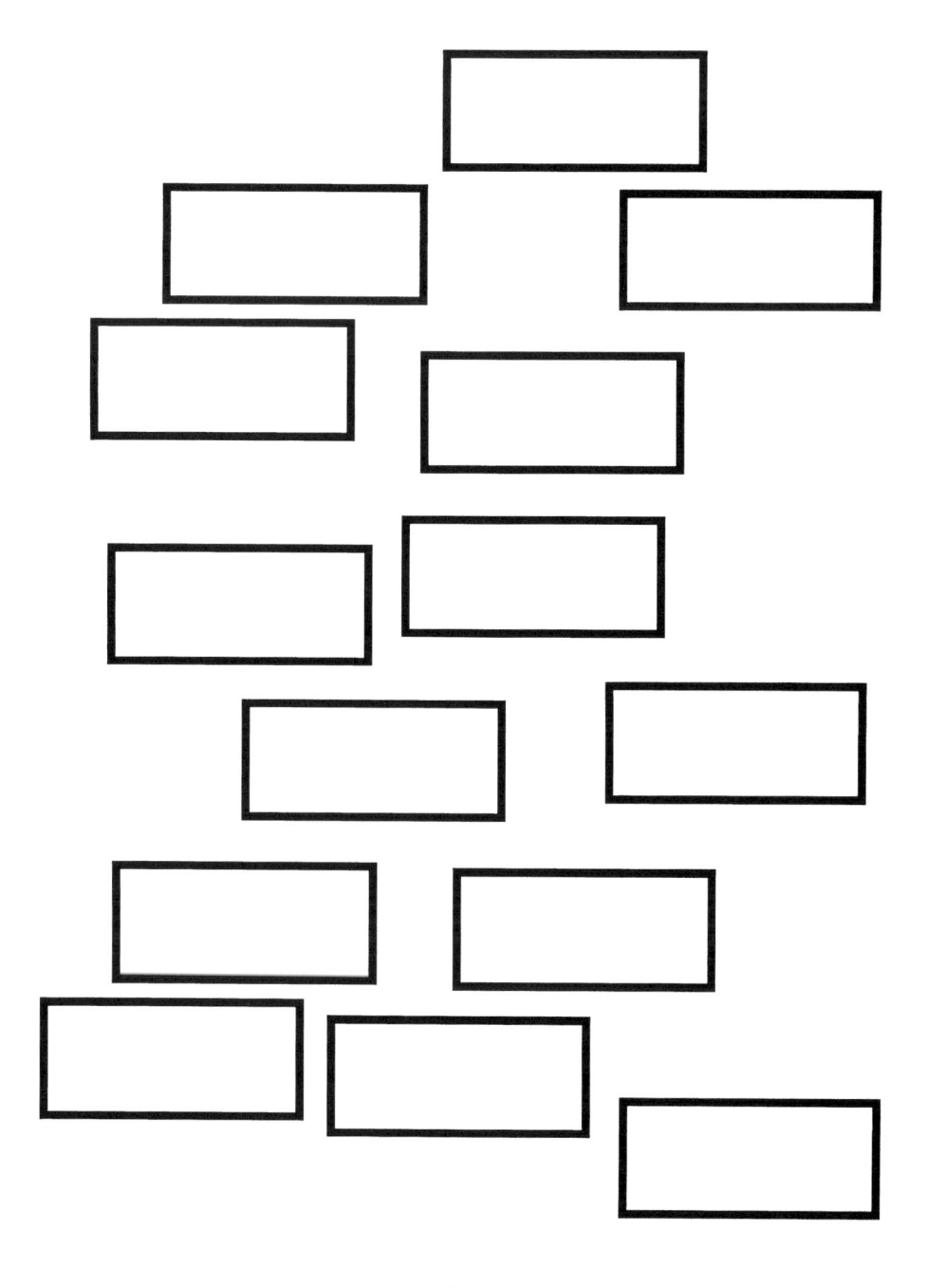

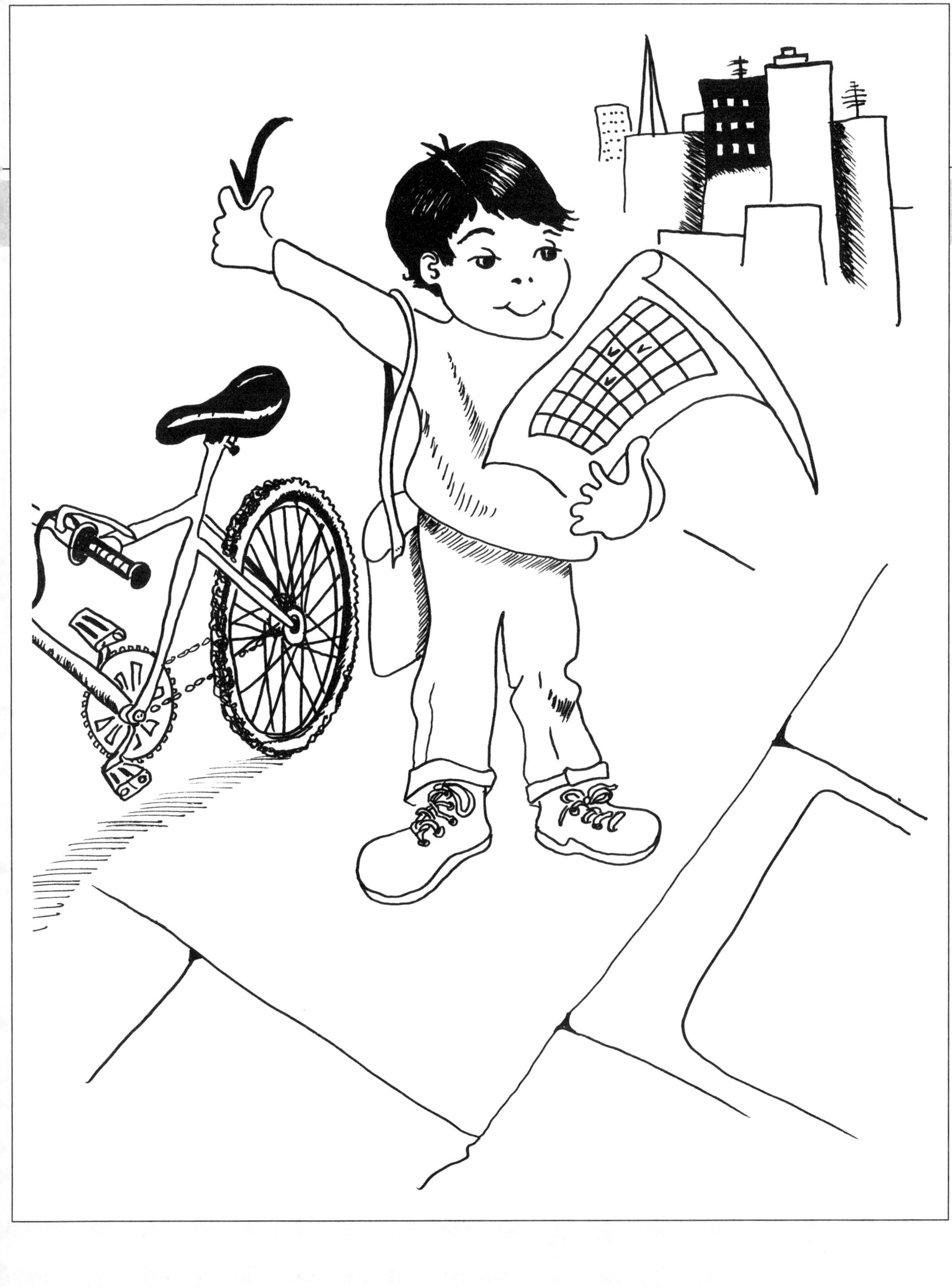

SECTION III

TOOLS FOR RECORDING DATA

CHAPTER 6

CHECK SHEETS
Keeping Track of Things

Many newspaper routes in Carlos's city were now motor or mail routes. The *Adelphi Announcer* delivered its papers mostly by truck or car. Carlos was among only a handful of young people still bringing the news by bicycle or on foot to neighborhoods. In some areas, customers got their newspaper by mail. They did not receive it until the next day.

Carlos wanted to do a good job with the route. He asked his route leader why the newspaper was not delivered by hand as much. Mr. Gomez said that the main reason was that it was so hard to find reliable delivery people. Young people did not seem to be interested. Sometimes they would not deliver on time or collect their bills when they were due. Carlos wanted to show Mr. Gomez that people his age could take their jobs seriously.

Carlos did not think that the hardest part of the job was delivering the papers. It meant getting up by 5:00 A.M. to get ready for his route, but he liked the early morning quiet once he was out on the road on his bike. Sometimes his dog Lucy would go with him, running alongside as Carlos pedaled. Carlos took pride in the job he did. He saw himself as a young businessman. He was actually buying the newspapers and selling them to his customers. The money that he collected included his own profit.

Collecting bills was important. If Carlos expected to make money at his job, he needed to bill his customers. He had to pay for the newspapers even if someone failed to pay him. Collecting bills was the hardest part of his job. With all his homework, it was hard to find time for it. His customers were usually not awake in the morning when he delivered the paper. Often they were not home after school or on weekends, either. Carlos had to make most of his collection calls in the early evening. During the winter, his parents worried about his safety, since it was often dark when he got back from his route. Also, he sometimes had to go back to the same house several times before finding anyone at home.

Carlos decided to look at the way he went about his collections. He wanted to improve the process if he could. (Remember: A process includes all the steps in something that is done.) He did not want to give up the route. However, he knew that unless he collected all the money that people owed him, he would not make a profit from his hard work.

One evening at dinner he shared his frustration with his family. He had gotten home late for the meal because he had been trying to collect. "Why don't you just quit that old job and mow lawns instead?" his younger brother said in disgust.

"Why don't you send your bills in the mail?" his sister suggested.

He thought about how much it would cost for postage. Carlos knew that this would not be a good solution. It would not really assure that people would pay. Besides, not all of his customers were hard to collect from. Many had their bills and money waiting when he knocked on their doors. Some of them gave him tips.

"Maybe you should collect all the information you can about who pays and when they are home," his mother offered. She knew that sometimes he returned to a customer's home time after time, only to find no one there.

Carlos thought about his mother's suggestion. He decided to write down the names of his customers. Next, he wrote the times they seemed to be available when he went to collect from them. The only information he really needed was when he was likely to find each customer at home. He knew the time periods when he usually collected. He

80 CHAPTER 6

Week:	1	2	3	4	5	6	7			
Monday	✔		✔			✔				
Tuesday	✔			✔	✔	✔				
Wednesday		✔		✔	✔					
Thursday	✔	✔	✔			✔				
Friday	✔		✔			✔				

FIGURE 6.1 Homework completed

decided that checking with each customer in those time periods would give good information. This information would be easy to track with a *check sheet*. He could also ask them about other times that they might be available.

Carlos had learned about check sheets at school. His teacher taught students to keep track of their own homework by checking every time they turned a homework assignment in on time. He looked at the check sheet he had used at school (Figure 6.1).

His teacher had mentioned that check sheets can take lots of different forms. They could have different numbers of rows (across) and columns (down). They might also have space for comments or other information. He decided to make a check sheet for his customers' available times. He also wanted more information than just the times he had collected from them in the past, such as other times they might be available. Carlos's check sheet was designed to give this information (Figure 6.2).

During his next round of collections, Carlos was able to collect data from most of his customers. For those who were not at home, he left a note asking them to write down the best times for him to return.

Carlos began to plan his collections around the schedules of his customers. His collection rates increased immediately. Besides, his frustration at returning again and again to try to collect disappeared almost entirely.

CUSTOMER NAME	CUSTOMER COLLECTION PREFERENCES										
	4-5 pm	5-6 pm	6-7 pm	7-8 pm	Sat. 9-10am	Sat. 10-11am	Sat. 11-12 n	Sat. 12-1pm	Sat. 1-2pm	Sat. 2-3pm	Sat. 3-4pm
Martinez	✓	✓						✓	✓	✓	
Gonzalez-Everhart		✓	✓				✓				✓
Moreno			✓								✓
Hart		✓	✓			✓	✓			✓	✓
Cruz		✓					✓	✓			
Hoback			✓					✓	✓	✓	✓
Muñoz	✓		✓	✓						✓	✓

FIGURE 6.2 Carlos's collection sheet (partial list of customers)

"I guess information can change things," Carlos said about the improvement he had seen.

SUGGESTIONS FOR USING CHECK SHEETS:

- The check sheet is meant to be used to collect data. It is useful because it is a way to record that data. The way it looks does not matter, as long as it does this.
- You can decide for yourself how much information you want on your check sheet. Make the columns (down) and rows (across) in such a way that you can record everything you want to record.

OTHER TOOLS YOU MAY USE WITH CHECK SHEETS

- Flowcharts, where information from a check sheet might show more about a certain step in the process

- Line graph, to visually show the data recorded on check sheets

- Fishbone or cause-and-effect diagrams, since check sheets can be used to keep track of causes

- Pareto or histograms, to show frequency of occurrence for each item

NAME: _____

CLASS: _____

DATE: _____

MY OWN THINKING TOOLS PAGE
CHECK SHEETS

First, Some Practice:

Make a list of the things you need to put into your backpack each day.

1. _____   8. _____

2. _____   9. _____

3. _____   10. _____

4. _____   11. _____

5. _____   12. _____

6. _____   13. _____

7. _____   14. _____

Now make a check sheet to help yourself remember to put all these things into your backpack (see Figure 6.3). Use the blank check sheet at the end of this chapter (or a copy of it). You may prefer to make your own check sheet on a separate piece of paper. Add this to your own thinking tools book.

Write the names of the items in the column down the left side of your check sheet. Across the top, write the days that you want to check your bag. This may be every day, or you may decide to check once a week. You might want to check your backpack only on Wednesdays, because you have discovered that you are more likely to forget things on Wednesday. There might be another period of time that will provide the information that you need. Remember that the check sheet should be useful, not just nice to look at.

How would a check sheet help Madison (chapter 1) with her science project?

Now It's Your Turn...

Create a check sheet reflecting your observation of weather, using the check sheet (see Figure 6.4). If you do not have access to weather instruments yourself, use the daily record that you find in the newspaper or on the radio to gather information.

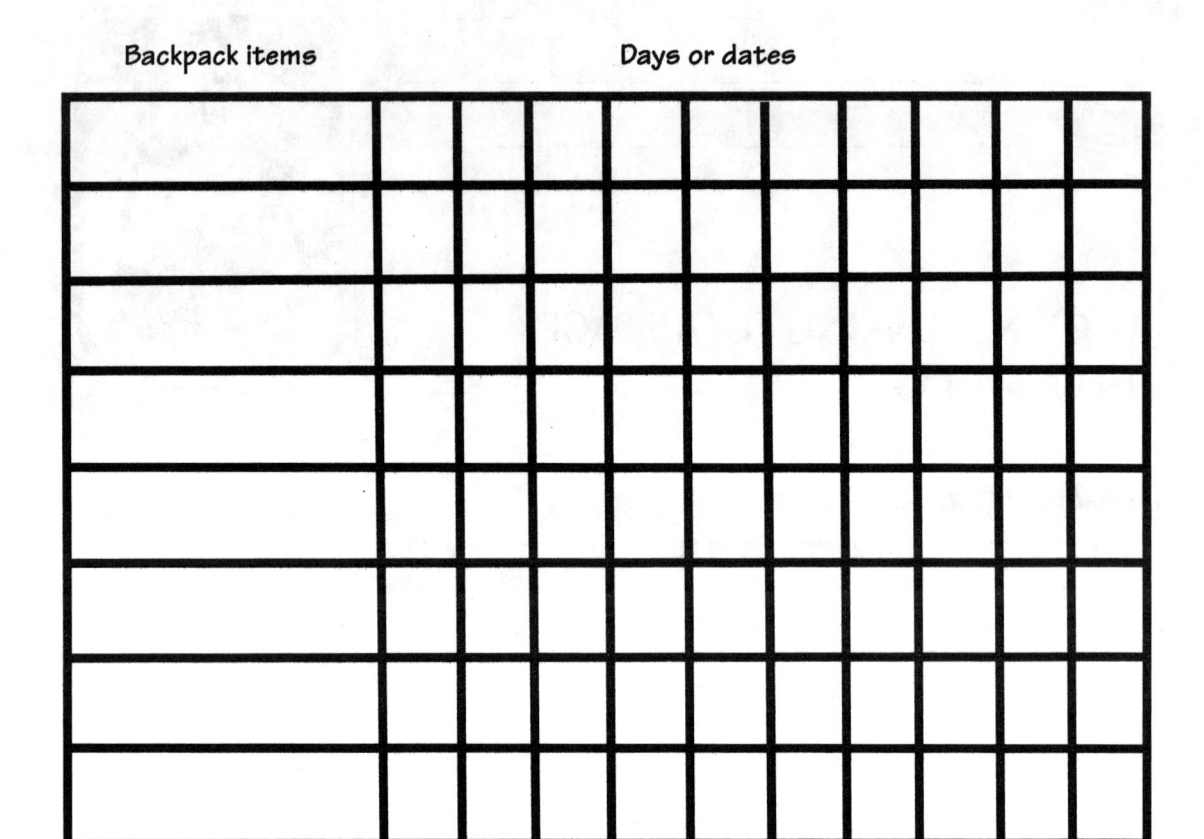

FIGURE 6.3 Backpack items

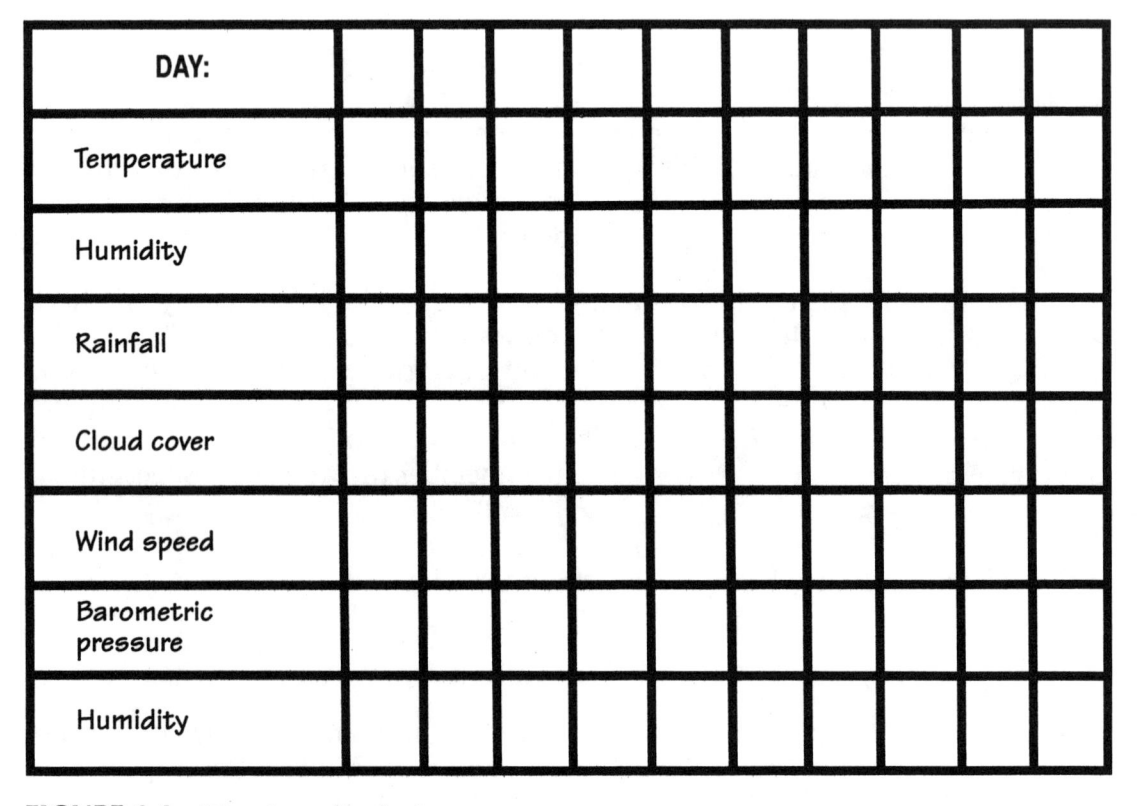

FIGURE 6.4 Weather check sheet

Other Possibilities

You can keep check sheets for many of your school tasks: homework, steps in a process, keeping track of lunch payments, and many others. A check sheet can be used by a group of people or an individual. Select one of the following ideas or one of your own, and keep data on a check sheet, either by yourself or with a partner.

1. Imagine that you have checked out several books from the library and want to keep track of when you have returned them so you can check out others. When you go to the library, write the names of the books on your check sheet. Write the date that each one is due. When you return it, check it off.

2. Your music teacher wants you to practice your trombone every day for at least 20 minutes. Write the days or dates across the top. In the lefthand column, write ranges of minutes that reflect your actual practice. For example, the first row might indicate "5–10 minutes," the second "11–15 minutes," and so on.

3. If you have a project that has many parts that need to be completed, use a check sheet to indicate that you have finished each part. If you are preparing a report for school, for example, you might write all the steps in the project in the lefthand column. Then write the dates that you expect to complete each stage across the top. As you complete each phase, you can check it off.

4. Keep a check sheet to help remember to do a regular chore that you may have in the classroom, such as feeding the gerbil, cleaning the erasers, passing out papers, or taking notes to the office. The tasks can be written across the top of the check sheet. Then students' names can be recorded down the lefthand column. Each time a student does his or her task, the student can put a check in the appropriate box. This is a good group project to help you learn about check sheets.

HOME CONNECTION

1. One of your weekly tasks at home is to water the plants. On a check sheet, write the days or times when the plants should be watered. Indicate each time you water the plants by putting a check in the box next to that time.

2. Keep track of your job of feeding your cat every morning or taking the trash out for your family. You might want to post your check sheet on the refrigerator so others can see how responsible you are!

3. Organize your shopping list for holiday gifts or family birthdays by using a check sheet.

4. Use a check sheet to be sure you have followed all the steps you need to do in any process. Making French toast is only one possibility.

5. Do you have a bad habit, such as not screwing caps on bottles carefully? (If you cannot think of one, just ask your parents!) Use a check sheet to keep track of the times you correct that habit.

NAME: _____

CLASS: _____

DATE: _____

CHECK SHEET TEMPLATE

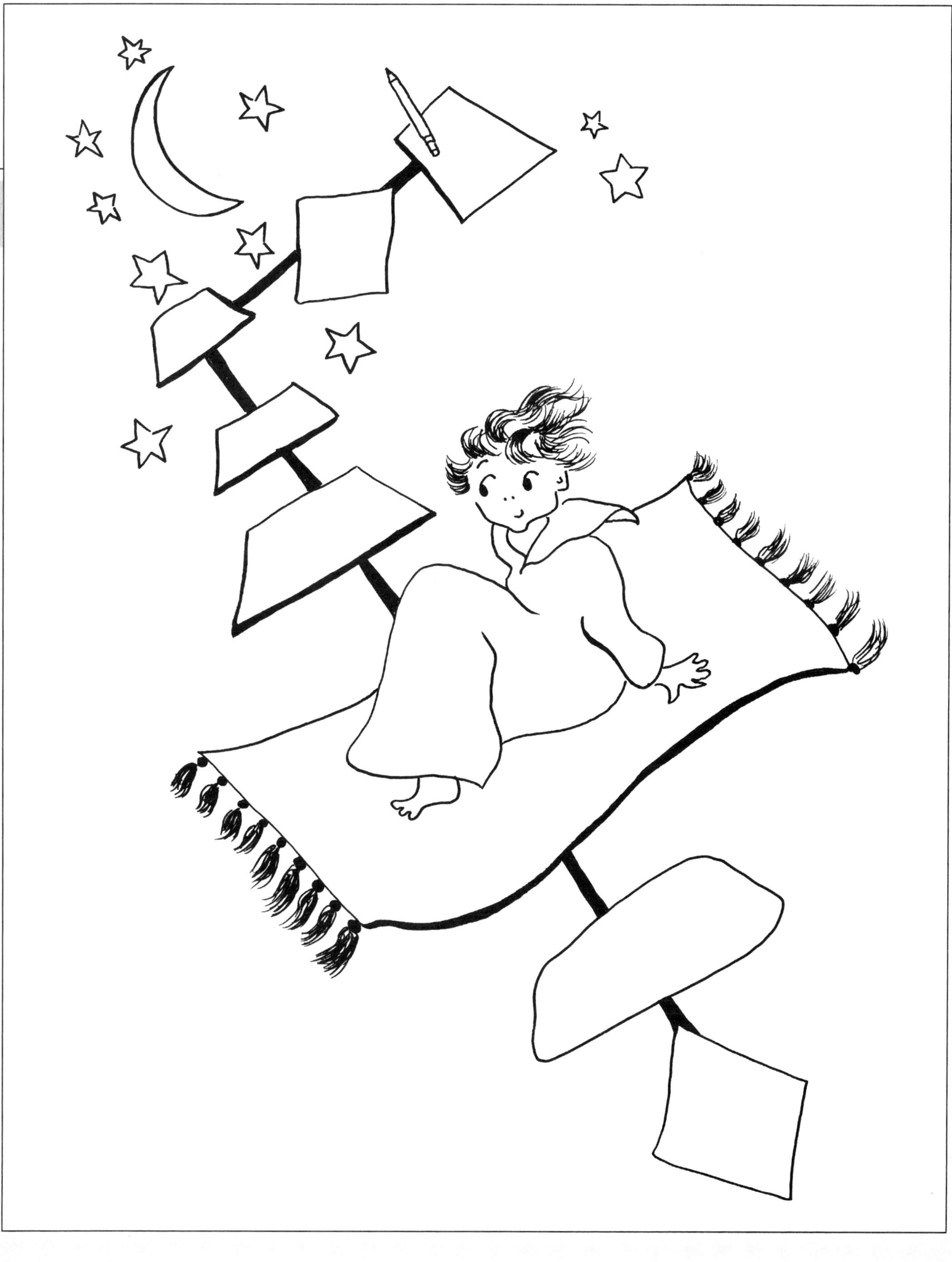

CHAPTER 7

FLOWCHARTS
Making Work Flow through Steps

Anya was having a hard time getting where she was supposed to be on time. She was often tardy to school. She showed up late after recess and lunch, and could not get her things together to go to the art room on time. Sometimes she missed her bus in the afternoon. Do you know anyone with this problem?

Anya *tried* to be on time. She wanted to be in her seat when the bell rang. She hated coming in late and facing her classmates and teacher after they had already started. She put her mind to improving and really concentrated, using her watch to be sure she knew the exact time. Usually, the result of this concentration was that her on-time performance was better for a day or two. But she always went back to her tardy ways. It's discouraging to keep trying and to see no real change. "I know I'm trying hard, but nothing happens," she said.

Because she was so discouraged, Anya was about ready to give up. Then she learned from her teacher about using problem-solving tools to improve. She decided to find out more about how to do this, and to use these tools to help herself get to school on time each day.

Before Anya could begin to make changes, she needed to understand exactly what the problem was. (Sometimes deciding exactly what the problem *is* is the hardest part of solving it.) She knew it wasn't her lack of trying. Talking it over with her teacher, she thought about her frenzy of activity each morning after she got up. "Maybe we can look at what you can do to get ready for school the night before," her teacher suggested.

"I guess I never thought about how the things I do before I go to bed can make me late to school," Anya said.

Her teacher taught her how to use a flowchart to show all the steps that were involved in getting to school. She learned that it wasn't just dawdling over her breakfast (as her mother thought) that made her late. Instead, it could have been a delay in any of the steps that led to her arrival at school.

She began to make a list of all the things she did in the process of getting ready to begin class that day. She remembered that staying up late to finish a project made her late for school once. So she listed the things she had done the night before, including the time she had after dinner, as well as in the morning.

- Finishing homework and projects
- Deciding what to wear

92 CHAPTER 7

- Setting the alarm clock
- Getting up
- Eating breakfast
- Getting dressed
- Finding books and book bag
- Making sure she had everything in her book bag
- Catching the bus
- Getting off the bus at school

Any one of these can affect Anya's tardiness to school, so they are related. They all contribute to the process of school arrival. They may not be in the exact order that Anya does them. She has written down everything she can think of that she does to get ready for school. Later, she can put them into order.

Anya's teacher told her that she could get information about her tardiness to school with other tools as well. A fishbone diagram (chapter 4) might help her focus on the reasons that she was late. After talking it over with her teacher, Anya decided that she first wanted a picture of the process. This is called a *flowchart*. Later, she might consider a fishbone diagram. That would help her figure out the "whys."

To make a flowchart for the process of school arrival, Anya had to learn flowchart symbols. These would make her chart understandable to someone else.

The symbols include a box for the beginning and for each of the steps in between. If a step involves a decision or a question, a diamond-shaped box is used instead. Figure 7.1 shows the drawing tools to use for a flowchart. They are also included at the end of this chapter. Ask your teacher to make copies of that page for you to use. Then you may want to color them (suggestions are listed in the figure).

If you want a larger flowchart, use construction paper or other larger sheets of paper for each of the symbols when you make your own flowcharts later in this chapter.

Figure 7.2 shows the flowchart that Anya made for getting to school. As she was making the flowchart, she began to realize that she was doing many of the activities in the morning instead of the night before. But she wrote them all down in the *order* that they usually took place, regardless of exactly when they were done.

By looking at Anya's flowchart, you can see the steps that she took to get ready for school. Many of the things we do every day also have steps, although we may not think about them this way. Flowcharts help to organize our thinking about the things that we do. Then we can reflect on how to do them better.

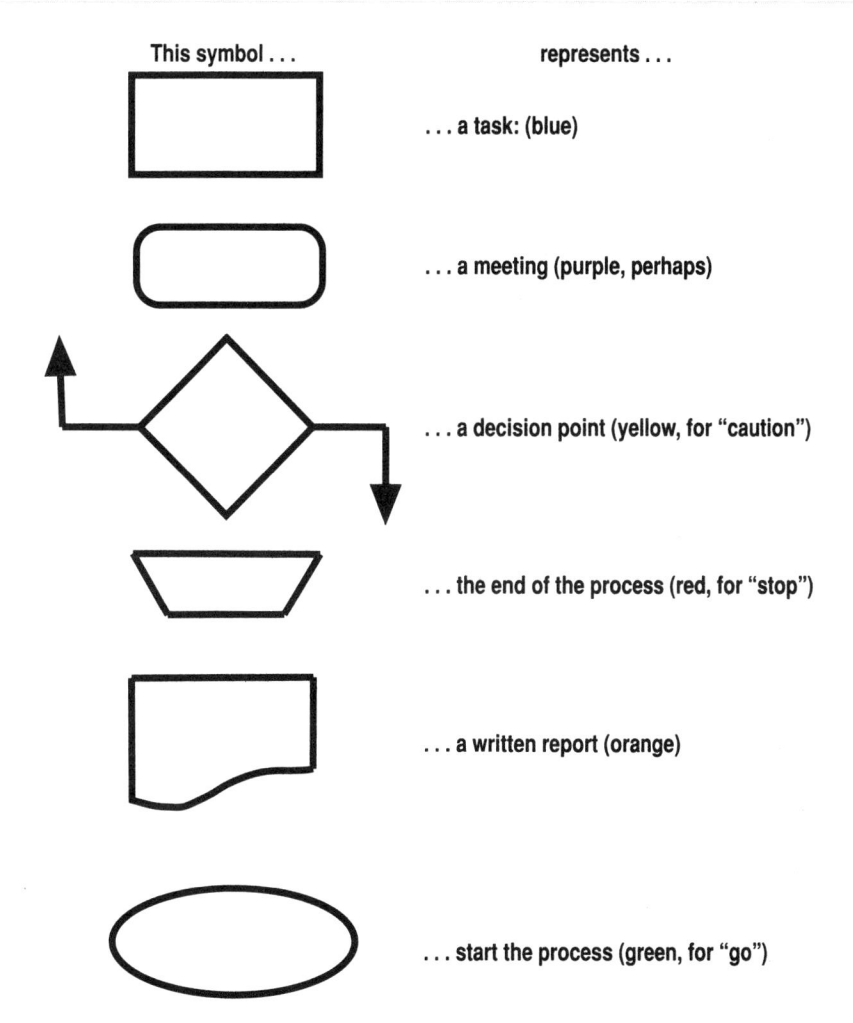

This symbol...	represents...
▭	...a task: (blue)
⬭	...a meeting (purple, perhaps)
◇	...a decision point (yellow, for "caution")
⏢	...the end of the process (red, for "stop")
🗎	...a written report (orange)
⬭	...start the process (green, for "go")

FIGURE 7.1 Symbols for flowcharts

One of the hardest parts of doing something that you repeat every day is figuring out the decision points. For Anya, this was also true. Knowing that a decision must be made involves really *looking ahead*. This is not always easy. In Anya's flowchart, her first decision point asks "Is homework finished?" If it is not, she must finish it. She may not actually have time to do that, though. If it is morning, for example, she will be late to school if she stops to do unfinished homework.

Anya looked at her finished flowchart. She realized that one of the reasons she was late was that she often did not finish her homework the night before. She decided that she needed to change her flowchart to show only the things she did the night before. Another flowchart might show her morning activities. By looking at the decision point in her original flowchart, Anya was able to see her problem.

Sometimes you do not realize that you are making a decision. You might ask yourself if it is snowing outside as you get ready for school. Depending on the answer to that question, you might put your boots on before you leave your house. In creating a flowchart to reflect a

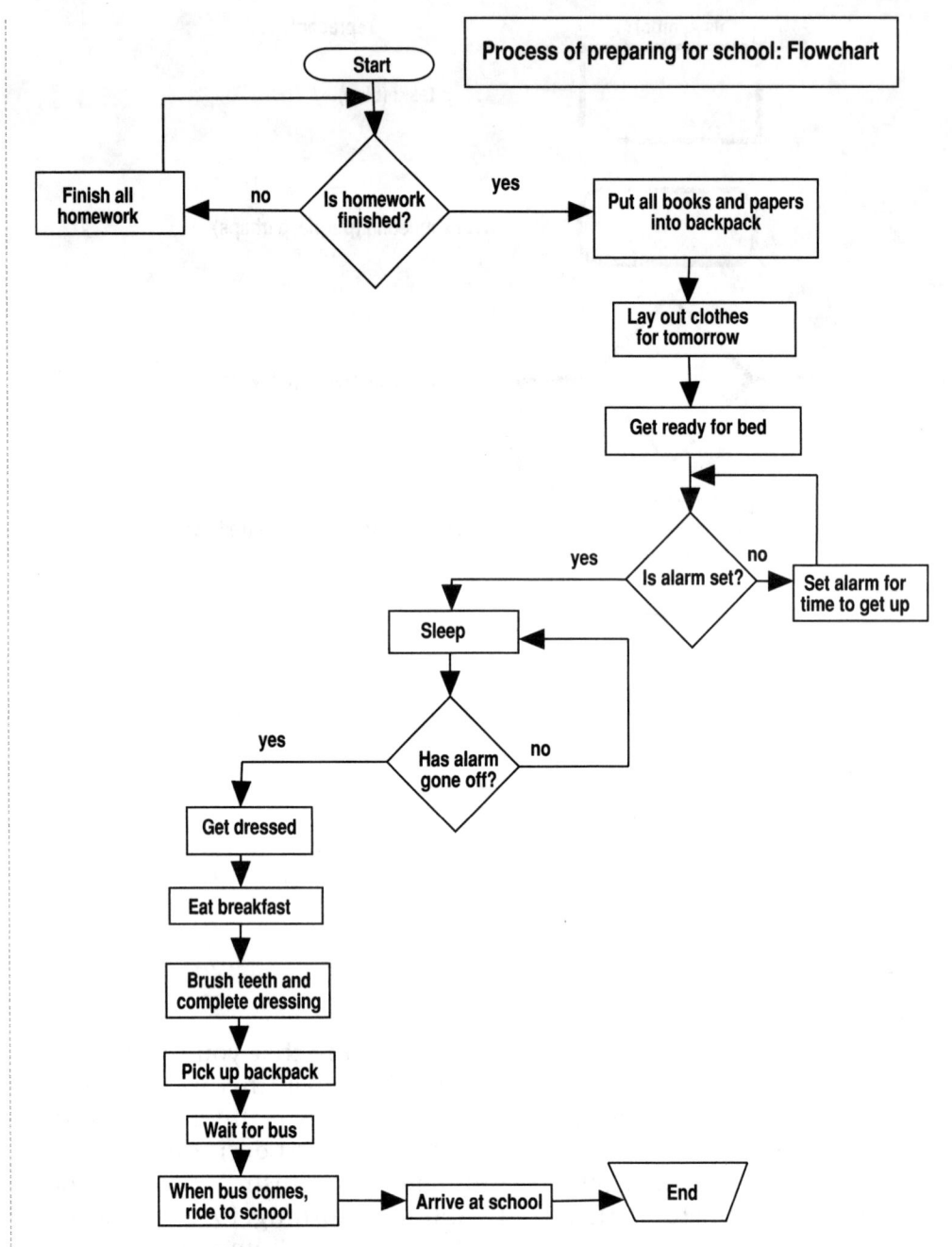

FIGURE 7.2 Anya's process flowchart

process (such as getting to school), it is important to think of the points where you must make a decision in order to take the right action. These decision points are shown on a flowchart as diamond-shaped boxes. A decision point may look like the one in Figure 7.3.

Anya decided that the flowchart was interesting to look at. Also, it had already shown what she could do to get to the classroom on time. Following her flowchart helped establish a discipline in getting ready for school. She even used it to keep track of when she did each task—morning or evening. By writing "A.M." or "P.M.," she could see whether

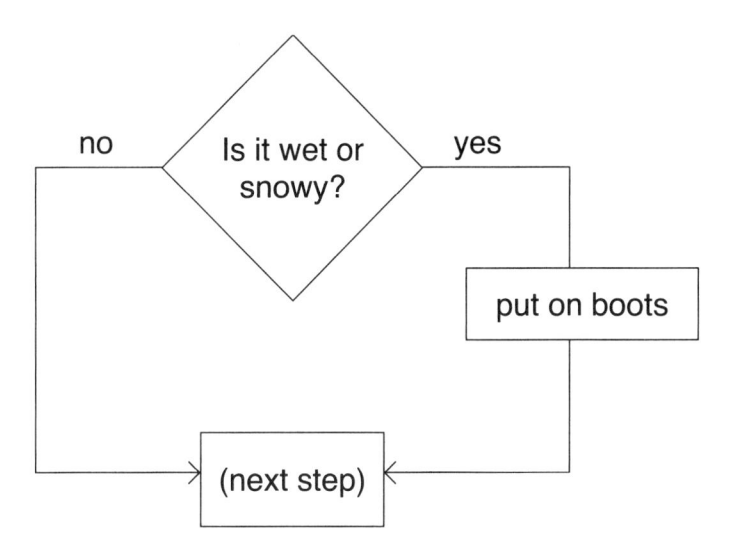

FIGURE 7.3 Decision point

```
Monday, May 4: on time (8:25).
Tuesday, May 5: Arrived 8:45. Overslept. Forgot to set alarm.
Wednesday, May 6: Arrived 8:35. Got to school on time.
Thursday, May 7: 8:40. Couldn't find homework after breakfast.
Friday, May 8: on time (8:23).
Monday, May 11: 8:36.
```

FIGURE 7.4 Anya's check sheet

the major portion of her preparation for school was morning or evening. The flowchart is a way of recording the following:

- Steps in a process
- Decisions to be made in that process
- Useful data about these steps if this is helpful

Since Anya needed to know even more about why she was late, she decided to write down a reason for being tardy on every day that she did not get to the classroom by 8:30. (This is the time that class started every morning.) This information would help her understand how often she was late. It would also give the reasons for each tardy. She decided to use her school assignment book to write it down every day. This would help her to remember to write her reasons.

Anya made a check sheet to support her flowchart. Her entries looked like those shown in Figure 7.4.

Her entries showed that there might be more that she could do to be on time. She was eager to try some ideas that she had for her own improvement. She saw that keeping track of her pattern of lateness was a good way to learn more about that pattern so she could change it. Then, she made a fishbone diagram to get further answers to the question of *why?* that she needed to answer.

Anya's story shows how several tools can go together to help understand something. She used a check sheet and a fishbone diagram in addition to the flowchart. As you make your own flowchart, think of other tools that would help you understand something better.

SUGGESTIONS FOR USING FLOWCHARTS:

- Walk through a process before your make your flowchart, taking notes as you do this.
- Make a first draft of your flowchart and try it out to be sure you have not forgotten any of the steps.
- Make a flowchart of the process *as it is,* rather than changing it as you go along. You can change it later, but your first purpose is simply to record the process in the form of a flowchart.
- Ask someone else to go through your process, using only the flowchart to do it. This is a good way to see if you have left anything out.

OTHER TOOLS YOU MAY USE WITH FLOWCHARTS

- Brainstorming, to think of all the steps you follow in a process

- Check sheets, to collect more information about a specific step in the process

- Fishbone, or cause-and-effect diagrams, to learn more about ways to improve your process

- Line graphs, to record data such as the amount of time that a process takes

NAME: _____

CLASS: _____

DATE: _____

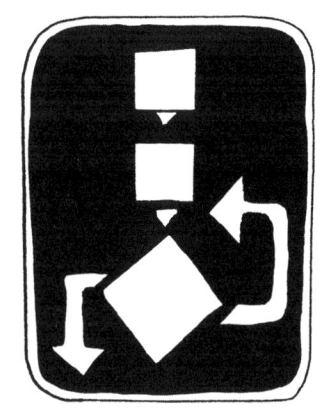

MY OWN THINKING TOOLS PAGE
FLOWCHART

First, Some Practice

This exercise gives you a chance to list the steps in a simple process—doing a crossword puzzle. You may do these steps in an order that is different from someone else's, but there will be some sequence in the way you do them.

Do the crossword puzzle in Figure 7.5, and as you're doing it, list the steps you take.

CLUES:

Across
1. I check these out from the library.
4. Myself (pronoun)
5. Leather baseball _____.
6. Opposite of "far"

Down
1. I sleep in a _____.
2. The Wizard of _____.
3. A female sibling
5. Gender. Not woman.

FIGURE 7.5 Crossword puzzle

Step by step, this is what I did to finish the puzzle:

1. _____

2. _____

3. _____

4. _____

Figure 7.6 represents a flowchart that shows all the steps you might have followed, in order:

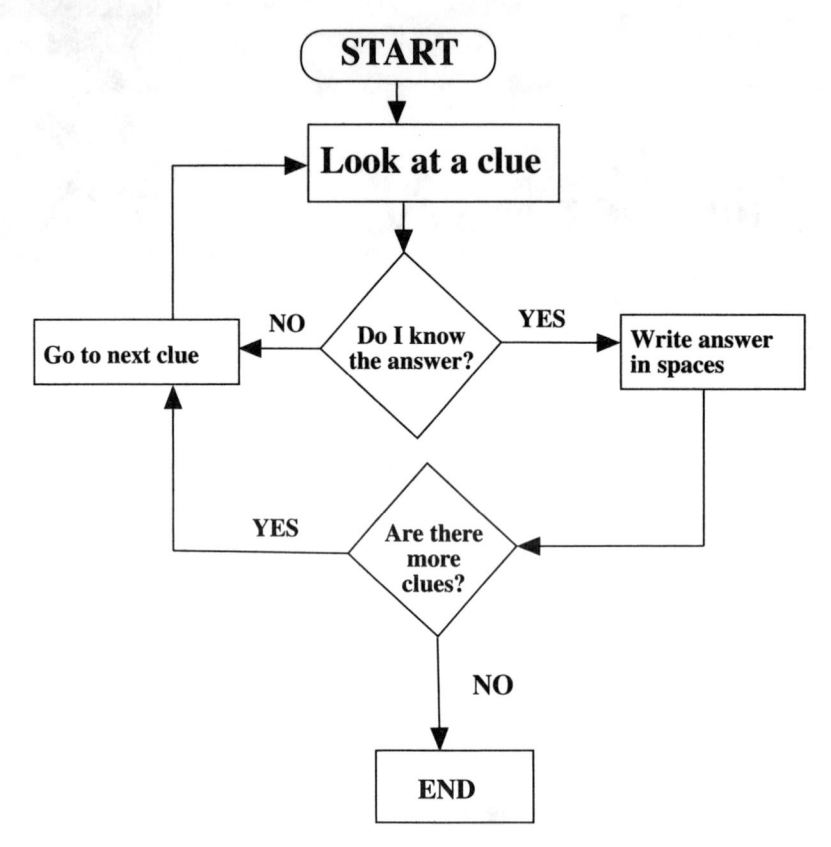

```
                    ┌─────────┐
                    │  START  │
                    └────┬────┘
                         ▼
              ┌─────────────────────┐
         ┌───▶│   Look at a clue    │
         │    └──────────┬──────────┘
         │               ▼
         │         ╱ Do I know ╲   YES    ┌──────────────┐
   ┌─────────┐ NO╱    the      ╲─────────▶│ Write answer │
   │ Go to   │◀──╲   answer?   ╱          │  in spaces   │
   │next clue│    ╲           ╱           └──────┬───────┘
   └─────────┘     ╲─────────╱                   │
         ▲                                        │
         │         ╱ Are there ╲                  │
         │ YES    ╱    more     ╲◀────────────────┘
         └───────╲    clues?    ╱
                  ╲            ╱
                   ╲──────────╱
                        │ NO
                        ▼
                   ┌─────────┐
                   │   END   │
                   └─────────┘
```

FIGURE 7.6 Crossword puzzle flowchart

Before you begin to make your own flowchart, Figure 7.7 shows one that Tommy used for making French toast (chapter 4, "Fishbone Diagrams"). You will see that the steps are written in order, using the symbols that were introduced to you in this chapter. How does this flowchart help you understand the process more clearly?

With a partner, decide on something you do at school each day, such as responding to a fire drill, working a particular kind of math problem (story problem, subtraction, multiplication, for example), returning a library book, returning from the cafeteria after lunch, or going to the gym during your physical education class. Make a list of the steps in that process, and together, make a flowchart that reflects it. (Your teacher or classmates may have some suggestions for other activities that you do in the classroom for you to practice making a flowchart.)

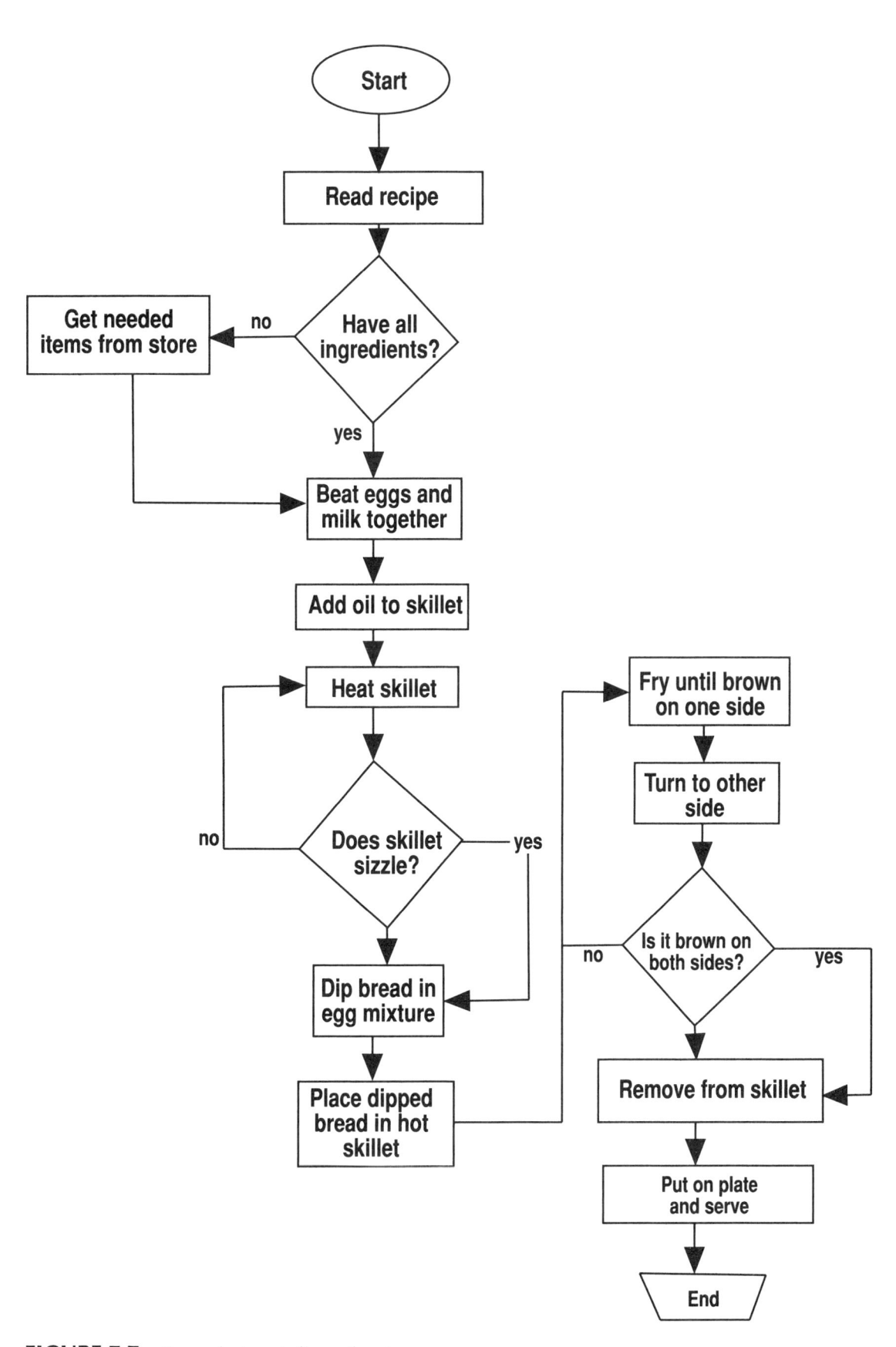

FIGURE 7.7 French toast flowchart

Steps in the process:

1. _____

2. _____

3. _____

4. _____

5. _____

6. _____

7. _____

8. _____

Be sure to identify the decision points in your process. If you are returning books to the library, the question "Are they overdue?" would direct your next action, because overdue books must be returned along with a fine, and books that are not overdue can simply be dropped into a return slot at the librarian's desk.

Draw your flowchart here, or use the symbols at the end of this chapter to make your flowchart. Remember to color the parts of the flowchart to make your picture even more helpful.

Flowchart for _____ (process)

Ask your partner to follow the flowchart you have created in order to check its accuracy. Is anything left out? Was it clear to you and your partner what to do next at each stage of the process? Make any changes in your flowchart that you think will make it easier to understand and follow.

Whenever you do something that has several steps, a flowchart can help you understand the process. It can also give you clues about how you can make it better. You may have found, for example, that your flowchart for library books showed an inefficient process. Maybe you can skip a step, or maybe there are other steps that should be added.

You can learn a lot about how you do things when you see a picture of the process.

Now It's Your Turn...

You do many different things each day in your class. Going to the library is just one example. What other processes are part of your school week? List them here.

1. _____
2. _____
3. _____
4. _____
5. _____
6. _____

Make a flowchart for one of those processes, either by yourself or with your partner. Use a large sheet of paper. What does the flowchart tell you about how you do the process?

_____
_____
_____

Ask your teacher to display all the flowcharts that your class has made and to leave them up so you can follow them as you go through your school day. Can you think of ways to change any of these flowcharts? Talk to your classmates about these changes.

Here's one for you to practice. Give a short *how-to* speech to your class. Teach your classmates how to do something you already know how to do, such as baking cookies, shampooing your dog, making a peanut butter sandwich, playing the flute, subtracting two digit numbers, or hitting a baseball. If possible, demonstrate the activity, and then illustrate it with a flowchart outlining all the steps in the process.

HOME CONNECTION

Think of all the steps in a process that you do every day, like setting the table or fixing your lunch or feeding your dog.

Like Anya, you have a step-by-step process for getting to school each day. Write down all the things that *you* do that contribute to your process of school arrival.

1. _____   11. _____
2. _____   12. _____
3. _____   13. _____
4. _____   14. _____
5. _____   15. _____
6. _____   16. _____
7. _____   17. _____
8. _____   18. _____
9. _____   19. _____
10. _____   20. _____

You may want to make two flowcharts for this process, as Anya did. Remember that she decided to make separate flowcharts for evening activities and morning activities. How does flowcharting help your process go more smoothly?

NAME: _____

CLASS: _____

DATE: _____

FLOWCHART TEMPLATE

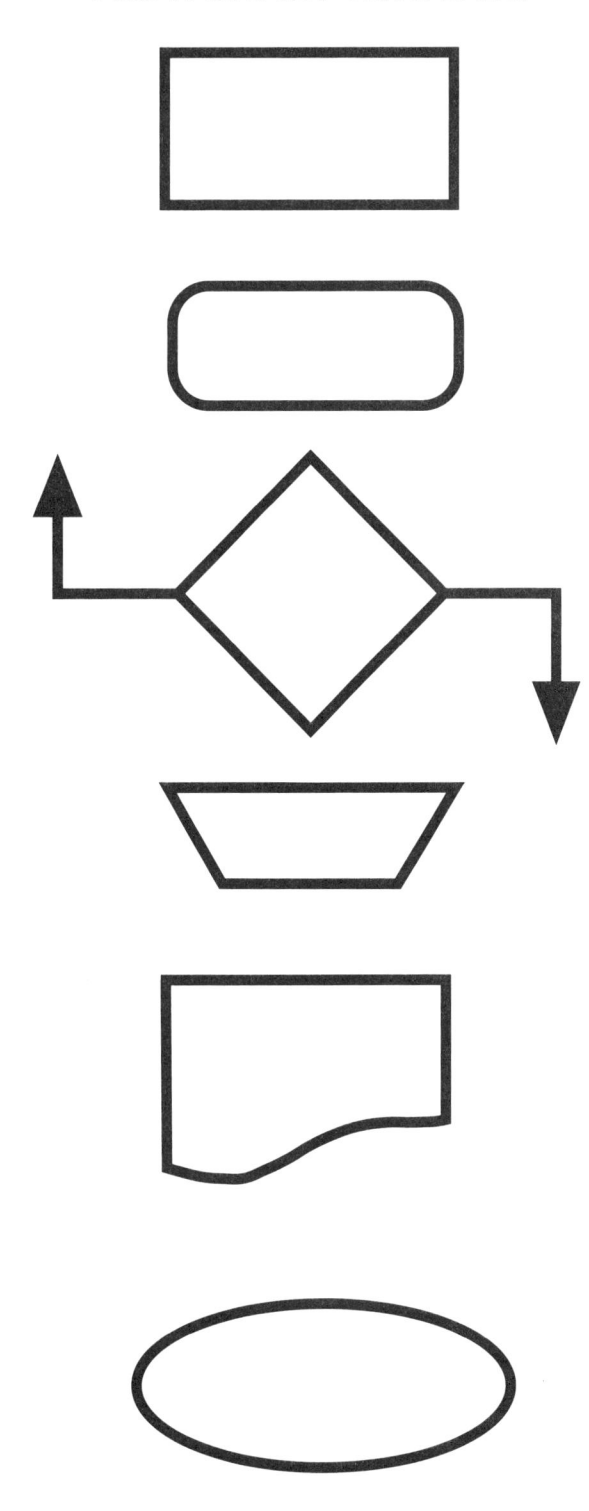

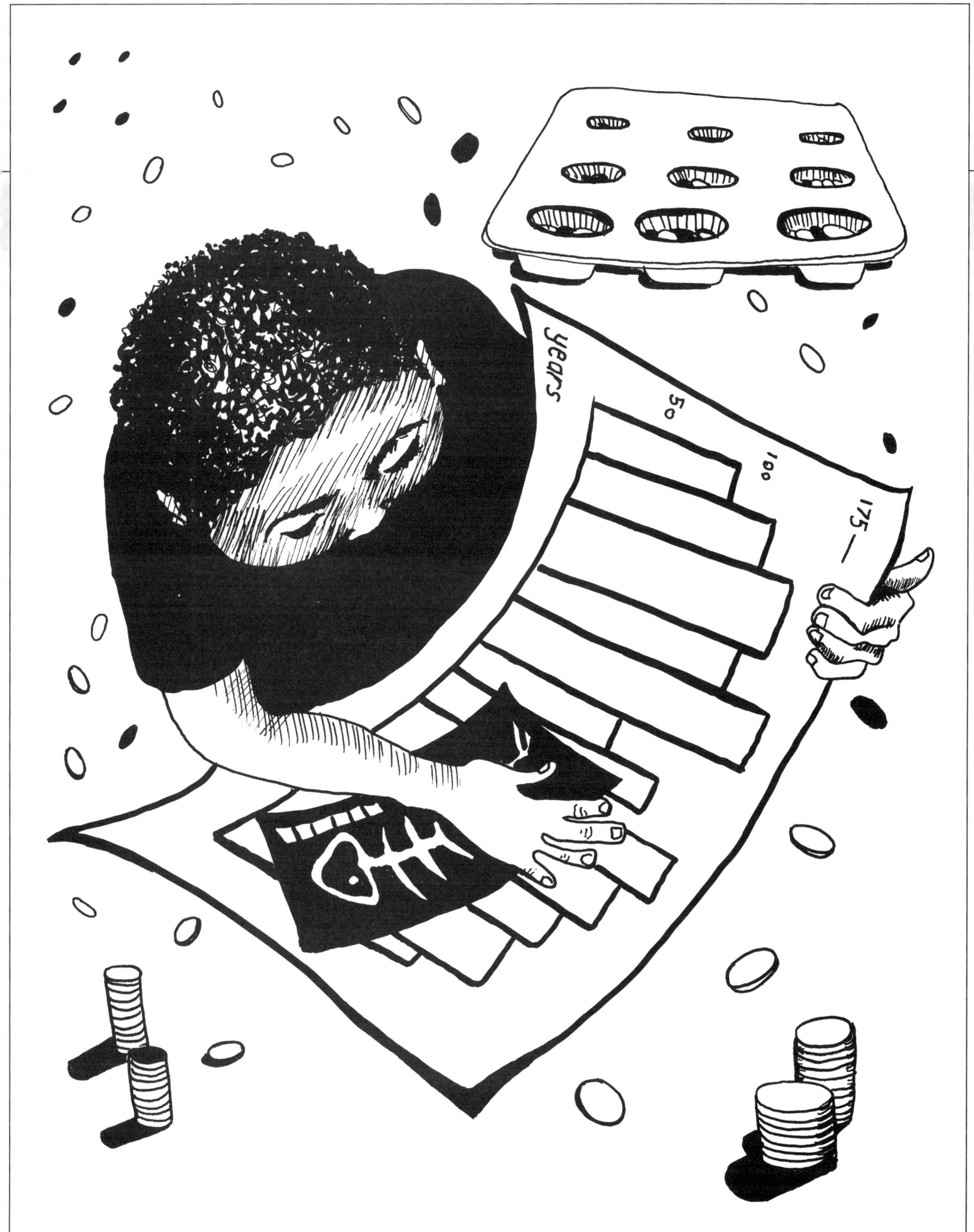
years
50
100
175

SECTION IV

TOOLS FOR SEEING PATTERNS

CHAPTER 8

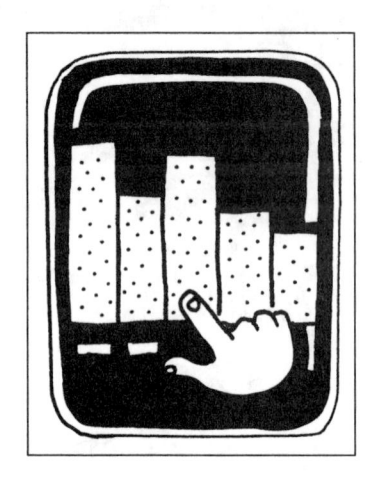

HISTOGRAMS: BAR CHARTS
Seeing Information with Your Own Eyes

Ariyah often went with his mother to visit elderly people at the Pavilion, a retirement center near their home. His mother was a volunteer who helped with activities for the residents. She led them in singing, played bingo with them, or helped with a simple craft activity. Ariyah would join in the songs or help pass out bingo cards for them. He had gotten to know some of them quite well, often looking forward to the visits. The old people looked forward to seeing him as well. The nurses said the residents were always a little disappointed when his mother came without Ariyah.

Mrs. Levy was one of their most enthusiastic participants, especially in the singing. One day when Ariyah and his mother arrived, they found that Mrs. Levy was ill and confined to her room. She would not be part of the group that day. The nurse said she would probably return the following week if she felt better by then.

Ariyah decided to go down the hall and visit Mrs. Levy while his mother was teaching the group how to make picture frames out of craft sticks. He asked the nurse if it would be all right. Nathan, the nurse, assured Ariyah that Mrs. Levy could have visitors. In fact, she had mentioned that she was sorry to miss seeing Ariyah and his mother this week.

Ariyah found Mrs. Levy sitting up in bed reading a magazine when he gently knocked on her door and went in.

"Oh, I'm so glad to see you," she exclaimed. "You were on my mind today."

She was easy to talk with. Ariyah found himself asking her about things he noticed in her room. Spotting a large iron pig, he carefully lifted it. It was heavy with coins. It was a piggy bank, Mrs. Levy explained, that she had had when she had been a child. "I really have no further use for it," she laughed, and asked if he'd like to have it.

"Well, I really can't—" he began. She insisted, so he said he'd ask his mother if it would be all right. He didn't want to take anything that she might want later. Just then, Ariyah's mother came in, looking for him. He had promised to turn the pages of her piano music for her, and it was time for singing. Mrs. Levy told her that she wanted to give Ariyah a gift, and they showed her the remarkable iron bank.

"If you get all those pennies out of the pig, you can report to me how many are there," Mrs. Levy added, winking at his mother. "I think they're older than I am, some of them, and I've been collecting them all my life." The three agreed that Ariyah would take the pig and keep it as a gift from the old woman. He would take all the pennies out of the pig and report back to her about the total amount. Ariyah was delighted. He loved counting.

When they got home, Ariyah ran to his room, eager to begin his project at once. Using a dinner knife from the kitchen, he began the difficult job of recovering the coins. He held the pig upside down, moving the knife up and down in the coin slot until pennies fell out a few at a time. Soon he had a giant pile of pennies. He counted them, but then he lost track of which ones he had counted. Ariyah would write down the number he had counted, then cross it out the next time he counted, and write down a new number. But he was confused and unsure about how accurate his counting was. He found himself recounting the entire pile.

"This is going to take forever," he reported to his mother when he went back downstairs. He had hoped to have a report about the pig's contents ready for Mrs. Levy when they visited the Pavilion later in the week. Now he felt discouraged about this. He realized that it would take a long time just to get the coins out of the pig. Counting would take even more time, especially if he had to keep recounting every time he got mixed up. Ariyah needed a way to make the process go faster in some way.

"Why don't you sort them as they drop out of the pig?" his father suggested. "You could make little bins for the years, and toss them into the right places as you go along. Then you can add up all the numbers from the small containers."

"You can use my muffin tins with the little cups in them," his mother said.

That seemed like a good idea, so after dinner Ariyah once again retreated to his room with all of his mother's muffin tins, and resumed the knife process. It went much faster when he only had to drop the pennies into the little cups without worrying about counting. He had labelled the cups with the names of the years. There might be some that dated from even before Mrs. Levy had been born, so he made labels starting in 1890 and going to 1985, when she had stopped collecting pennies. He wanted to be able to add all the years up to find the total number of pennies in the iron pig.

Ariyah sorted the pennies into piles of dates, and when he was finished sorting, he counted the number in each section of the muffin tins. He had to empty the tins into other containers as they got full. These were also labeled, so he had large piles for every year.

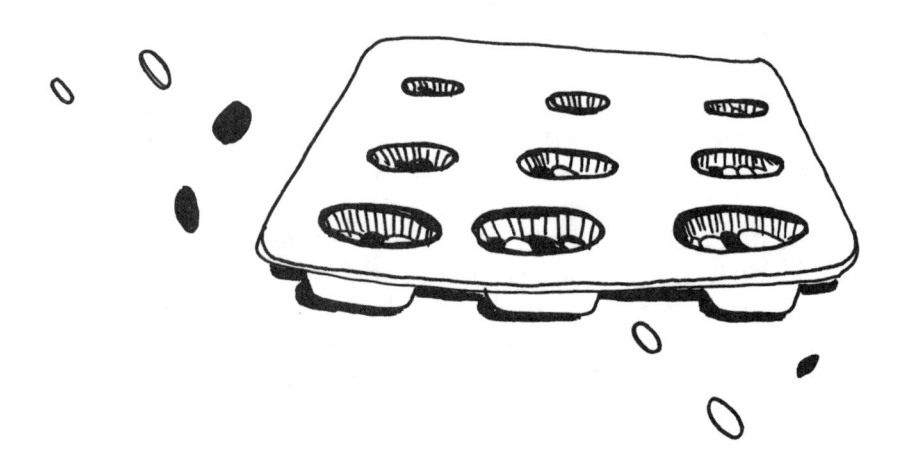

He found himself having fun with the pennies. He kept thinking of different ways to organize them and to get more information about the collection. His class had learned about different kinds of thinking tools at school, and he wanted to use the pennies to practice some of these tools. He wondered how many pennies were made by the United States mint in each year. Ariayah checked the almanac for that information. He found that different years had different numbers of pennies minted. He decided that after he had counted the pennies, he would make a *line graph* (chapter 9) to see the pattern that the years made. He could also create a *Pareto chart* (chapter 10) that would show which years had the greatest numbers of pennies. All of these tools would give him charts to show to Mrs. Levy. She would love to see how much information he gained from the iron pig and its pennies.

Finally, Ariyah counted the pennies in each pile and added them all together. There were more than 5,000 pennies there. He could hardly wait to tell Mrs. Levy. Her pennies added up to $51.63. That was too much money for a gift, so Ariyah took the pennies back to Mrs. Levy.

When he went back to the Pavilion, Ariyah told Mrs. Levy about the number of pennies. Several of her friends wanted him to count the coins in their collections, too. He spent the afternoon visiting their rooms and counting. Mrs. Levy's friends had pennies or other coins in boxes, jars, bags, and banks. Some of the Pavilion residents collected nickels or dimes. Most of them had penny collections like Mrs. Levy's. Other containers were easier to empty than Mrs. Levy's iron pig had been. Ariyah liked the banks with rubber stoppers in the bottom. He could quickly dump the coins, count them, and put them back. Two gentlemen told Ariyah to take their coin boxes home and count them. He could bring them back the following week, they said.

When he got home, Ariyah finished counting the other coin collections. He kept track of the numbers by using a check sheet (Figure 8.1).

Less than $10		$30-31.99	/
$10-11.99		$32-33.99	///
$12-13.99		$34-35.99	///
$14-15.99		$36-37.99	//
$16-17.99	//	$38-39.99	////
$18-19.99		$40-41.99	/
$20-21.99		$42-43.99	//
$22-23.99	/	$44-45.99	
$24-25.99	//	$46-47.99	
$26-27.99	///	$48-49.99	/
$28-29.99		$50-51.99	/

FIGURE 8.1 Amounts in everyone's collections: Check sheet

Each time he went back, other residents had heard about Mrs. Levy's penny collection. They wanted Ariyah to help them count their collections, too. It was a kind of game. They all wanted to see who had the most coins in their collections. Finally, he had counted more than 25 collections of coins. He decided to make a *histogram* to show all the different collections that people had given him to count.

A histogram is also known as a bar chart. After the sorting was complete, Ariyah's check sheet showed the number of pennies (or other coins) in the collections he had counted. He used this check sheet to make his histogram. Along the side of the histogram are numbers to show how many of the collections contain the amounts on the bottom of the chart. Those amounts are ranges, or groups of numbers, that reflect the piles of coins. These will become the bars for the histogram. He had exact data for each of the residents, but his chart showed the pattern that all their collections made.

At first, Ariyah did not know what numbers to put along the bottom. His teacher taught him how to *scale* the histogram, or divide the numbers so they made sense. (Rules for scaling histograms are given in the Glossary.) Some of the groups on his check sheet were empty, so he combined them according to the rules for scaling, and made his histogram (Figure 8.2).

When Ariyah showed the histogram to Mrs. Levy, she looked at it carefully. "I guess that $51.63 is a big amount, especially when you see

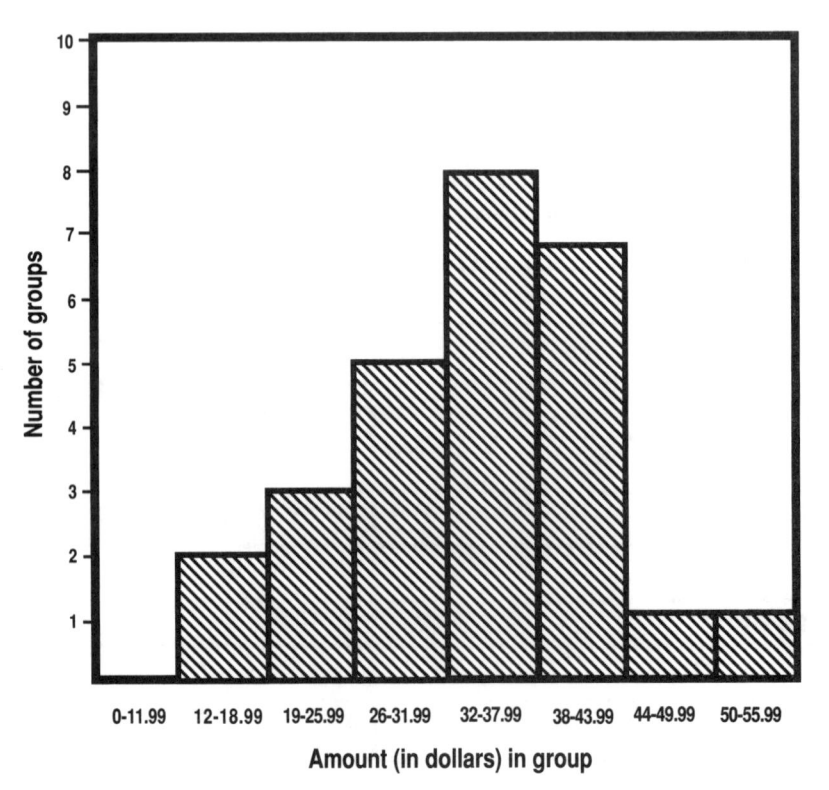

FIGURE 8.2 Amounts in everyone's collections: Histogram

all those pennies," she said. "You know when I was a child, 5 pennies was a lot of money." Together they were able to analyze the histogram. Mrs. Levy said she thought it was really something to see how many people had coin collections. Most of her friends had put away coins, some collecting them longer than others.

Ariyah learned a lot by making his histogram. He learned even more by talking about it with Mrs. Levy.

A histogram is useful when you want to know how many items fall along a continuous line. The line may show size, volume, amount, or other information. It looks a little like a Pareto diagram (chapter 10). Histogram bars show where individual items fall on a continuous line. The groups are not arranged on the chart by their size. Instead, the line on the bottom shows something that gradually gets bigger. This is called a *continuum*. A continuum is different from categories, since the line keeps going, by time or size or some other measure, in a continuous sweep. (A category might be a color, or an individual year or month, for example.) Ariyah's penny groups were arranged by the number in the collections. He could see how many collections had smaller numbers and how many had larger numbers.

At Ariyah's school, the school nurse keeps a check sheet. It shows when children come to the office. He also writes the amount of time he spends with each child. Then he makes a histogram to reflect how much time it takes to serve each child. Along the bottom of the chart are times, by minutes. Each time a child comes to his office, the nurse notes how much time it takes to treat that child, and then makes a histogram to show this data (Figure 8.3). On the left side of the chart are the numbers of children that come into the office for care.

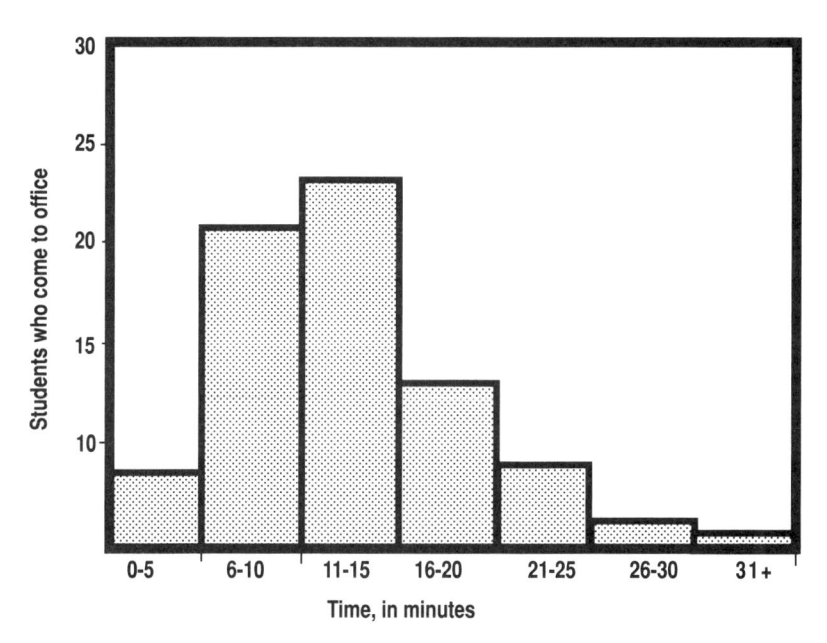

FIGURE 8.3 Visits to the nurse's office: Histogram

This chart shows that most treatments take between 10 and 15 minutes. Very few involve the nurse's time for more than 30 minutes.

A histogram, like other graphs, gives a *picture* of data. Looking at this picture helps you understand the data. For Ariyah, the numbers in each pile were only numbers until he made the histogram. Then he was able to see a pattern.

Collecting data for a histogram also made Ariyah think about other ways to use the data. He thought of several tools he might use for further analysis. Thinking tools can help to solve problems. They can give information about your data. Information helps you to think about something. One way to think is to ask questions. What other questions would you ask about Ariyah's histogram?

Ariyah used his histogram to give information to Mrs. Levy about her penny collection and those of her friends. It also helped him to learn some things he had not guessed he would learn. Did you know that some pennies made during war time were stainless steel instead of copper?

SUGGESTIONS FOR USING HISTOGRAMS

- Be sure to determine the number of groups by counting the number of data points. (For Ariyah, this was the total number of coin collections that he counted for Mrs. Levy and her friends.)
- Use a scale for the left axis that makes the most sense. Follow the rules that Ariyah used, for the most accurate scale. These rules are given in the Glossary.
- When you make a histogram, you may want to color each bar in a slightly different way. This helps to tell the difference between them.
- You can get creative with your histogram, too. If you are making a chart of pennies like Ariyah's, you can draw stacks of pennies instead of bars. How about stacks of hamburgers? Or different pets? Be sure your drawing is related to your subject for the histogram.

OTHER TOOLS YOU MAY USE WITH A HISTOGRAM

- Check sheets, to keep a tally of your data

- Fishbone diagrams, to get to the *why* of your data

- Line graphs, to show a pattern of the data in time order

NAME: _____

CLASS: _____

DATE: _____

MY OWN THINKING TOOLS PAGE
HISTOGRAM

First, Some Practice

Collect data about the age range in your classroom. Usually, all the students in a classroom are within a year or two of each other's ages. You can see if this is true for your class.

Find out the ages of your classmates, in months. If Krista is 10 years old, for example, she would be 120 months old (10 years times 12 months). But this is true only if her birthday is during the current month. If her birthday was last month, she would be 121 months old, for example. If Krista's birthday is next month, and she will be 10 on that birthday, she would be 119 months old right now (9 years times 12 months, plus another 11 months).

Use the check sheet in Figure 8.4 to write down the ages of your classmates. Record the ages (in months, remember) on the left, and then tally the number in each group. You may prefer to make your own check sheet to be sure you have enough rows for your own data.

How many of your classmates are the same age as you are, in months?

AGES	TALLY OF NUMBERS FOR EACH AGE GROUP
EXAMPLE: 100 MONTHS	⦀⦀ ⦀⦀ ⦀⦀⦀⦀

FIGURE 8.4 Gathering data for histogram with check sheet

Then, make a histogram from this data. Use the blank chart at the end of this chapter, or ask your teacher to make a copy of it for you to use for this exercise.

For more practice with information about your classmates, measure everyone's heights, in inches. Use a check sheet to record the data. Your check sheet might look like Figure 8.5.

Count the number of classmates you have measured, and decide how many groups you want to have from this number. Remember this general guideline:

Fewer than 50	Use 5–8 groups
50–100	Use 6–10 groups
100–250	Use 7–12 groups
More than 250	Use 10–20 groups

Across the bottom of the chart, write the groups that you have decided to use. These might be ranges of heights (36–40 inches, for example) or single heights in inches. This depends on the total number of students you have measured.

On the left side of the chart, make a scale by using this method: Find the number in the largest group, and subtract from it the number in the smallest group. Then divide that number by the number of groups you have decided to use. For example, in Figure 8.4, the greatest number in a group is 18. The smallest is 2. Subtract 2 from 18. Then divide that number (16) by the number of groups, which is 7, getting 2.2. You will want to use a scale with increments of 2 or 3. The reason for all this figuring is to be sure that your data will all fit on the chart.

Height	Tally of numbers
38 inches	𝍷𝍷𝍷𝍷𝍷 ΙΙ
39 inches	𝍷𝍷𝍷𝍷𝍷 𝍷𝍷𝍷𝍷𝍷
40 inches	𝍷𝍷𝍷𝍷𝍷 𝍷𝍷𝍷𝍷𝍷 𝍷𝍷𝍷𝍷𝍷
41 inches	𝍷𝍷𝍷𝍷𝍷 𝍷𝍷𝍷𝍷𝍷 𝍷𝍷𝍷𝍷𝍷 ΙΙΙ
42 inches	𝍷𝍷𝍷𝍷𝍷 ΙΙΙΙ
43 inches	ΙΙΙΙ
44 inches	ΙΙ

FIGURE 8.5 Tallying numbers for histogram of heights

Next, make a histogram showing the pattern of the heights in your classroom. When you look at the check sheet (Figure 8.5), you can see how the tally marks already suggest a histogram. More children are 41 inches than any other height. Use the blank chart at the end of this chapter and make a histogram using the height data.

One of the things you may notice when you look at the histograms for age and height is the pattern on the chart. For Ariyah and his pennies, the chart had no real pattern because it was a random collection of piles of coins.

The pattern you see may be a kind of mountain in the middle of the chart, like Figure 8.6.

This pattern is called a *bell curve* because some people think it looks like a bell. It is also called a normal curve. You may find other kinds of patterns. This depends on what you are analyzing. The bell curve shows more data in the middle of the groups than at the ends. If you are measuring heights, you can see why this would happen. Most of your classmates are no more than several inches shorter or taller than you are, for example. Why would this be the case? If you were writing down ages in your class, do you think you would find a bell curve in the chart?

It is sometimes useful to see the curve (or distribution) in order to make good decisions about something. Pretend you are planning a field trip to an amusement park, for example. It would be nice to know how many children are tall enough to go on rides that require a certain height. Can you think of other reasons for knowing the pattern of heights among your classmates?

FIGURE 8.6 Normal distribution on histogram

Now It's Your Turn...

Anytime you make a histogram, you must collect data. Here are some suggestions for collecting data.

1. Maximum temperature each day
2. Distances that students travel to school
3. Distances that a ball is thrown by students
4. Numbers of student absences in your school
5. Number of televisions in each of your neighbors' homes
6. Number of books that students have read for book reports
7. The ages of pets that people in your school have
8. Number of years of musical instruction that students in your school have had
9. Amount of rainfall or snowfall (daily) during a month or a season
10. How many states students have visited
11. How long classmates have lived in your town or state
12. How many minutes of recess in your school

What ideas do you have? List some ideas for collecting data for histograms.

1. _____
2. _____
3. _____
4. _____
5. _____
6. _____

With a partner, collect data for one of these ideas. Use a check sheet to gather the information that you will need. Then make a histogram to show how many are in each group.

HOME CONNECTION

Whenever you collect data, you begin to see things differently. A pattern gives you more information. You can use this information in different ways. It can help you to make comparisons. You might make histograms of the ages of your classmates and another for the ages of another class. If you look at these two charts, the numbers will be different, but the patterns that they make may be similar. This is an interesting profile of your class.

Here are some other things you can study at home. Collect data in the same way you did with your partner at school. Then make a histogram from that data.

1. How many minutes each person in your family spends talking on the phone each evening
2. Number of seeds in each of the apples in a half bushel
3. How many food items from each nutrition group (e.g., fruits, vegetables) that members of your family have eaten each day
4. Shoe sizes among all your friends and relatives
5. Survey of the number of ice cream cones people in your neighborhood have eaten in a given week
6. Miles per gallon of gas per tankful in your car
7. Time to drive from home to work or school
8. How long it takes for you to do your chores each day
9. Number of raisins in your cereal each morning
10. Time it takes for everyone in your swimming class to swim a length of the pool

NAME: _____

CLASS: _____

DATE: _____

HISTOGRAM TEMPLATE

Histogram title:_____

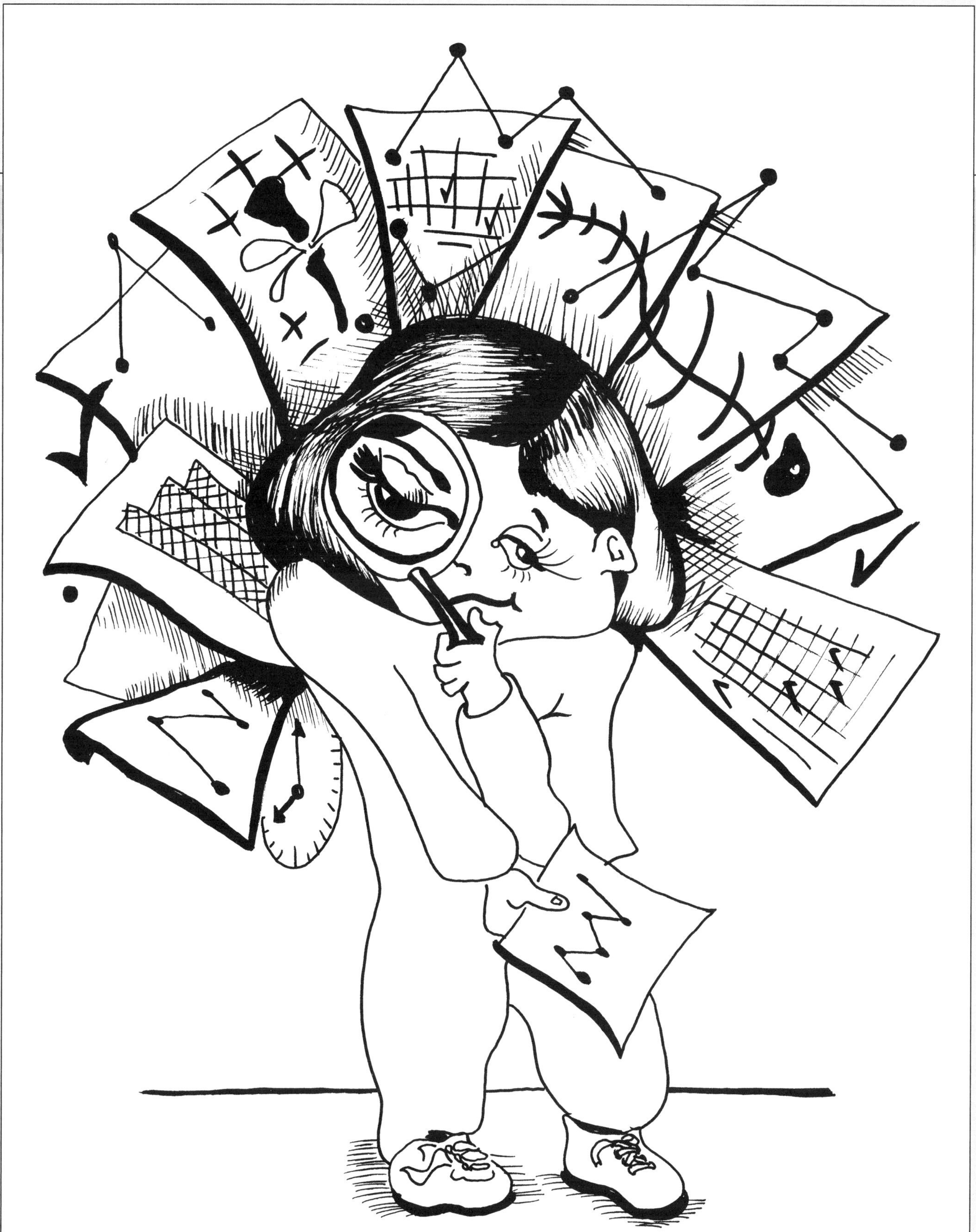

CHAPTER 9

LINE GRAPHS
Changing Numbers into Information

Erin was an avid reader. She loved mystery books in particular, reading everything from *Ramona* to *Nancy Drew* and the entire *Hardy Boys* series. She often thought of herself as a kind of detective. She was good at solving problems and finding things that were missing. She could also be a newspaper reporter, she thought, seeing things that others might miss. Her family could always count on her help when they had lost things—something that often happened in her family. Her father had lost his car keys one day and had turned the house upside down to find them. Then Erin traced the steps he had taken when he had last used the keys. She remembered that he had picked up the mail, then made himself a glass of iced tea before sitting down to sort the mail. Erin found the keys on top of the refrigerator, where he had laid them when he was getting ice from the freezer.

Erin's family said that she collected information the way some kids collect stamps. Alert to everything that was going on around her, she would record facts and things she saw on little slips of paper or write them in a small notebook she carried with her. The trouble was that she sometimes seemed to have a great deal of information that had no meaning to her. For example, she had written down the times that her neighbor, Mr. Gunther Badgekar, had backed out of his driveway each morning to go to a school in the distant town where he taught. The numbers, she knew, were what is known as *data,* or simple facts that had no meaning in themselves. Data could be numbers or words, not connected to anything else. In order to really have information, one must look at data and think about it more.

Erin had a complete set of data about Mr. Badgekar and his daily departures for nearly a month: 8:12, 8:15, 8:06, etc. She was interested in the data because it was a collection of her observations. Other than that, she did not know how it might be useful. It was just a list of numbers, after all. "But," she told herself, "if there were ever a crime committed at the Badgekar residence, I would be a great help to the police." She knew that the chances of this were slim, except for people like Nancy Drew. She decided that she needed to have a greater sense of purpose in collecting information.

To search for ways to make her data more useful, Erin went to the teachers' section of her school library. She came across a book that showed techniques to help children learn. The book described a number of ways to organize data to make it easier to understand. Erin saw all kinds of charts, including line graphs (also called run charts), pie charts, histograms, and Pareto charts. She did not know what these were, but they looked like something that would help her. She checked the book out and began to study it.

Beginning with line graphs, Erin decided to practice with the data she had collected about Mr. Badgekar. Following the directions given in the book, she wrote "dates" across the bottom of the chart. Then she wrote the times down the left side. "Dates" were the days when she had written down departure times. The times were what her clock said when Mr. Badgekar left his driveway. Since he left within the same half-hour period each day, she decided to break the times down into 15-minute spaces for the chart. Figure 9.1 shows the chart before she recorded any information.

Erin was using data already written down. She only had to look in her notebook to find the numbers to put on the chart. She noted each day's time with a dot at the point above its date. Then she connected the dots. This reminded her of the connect-the-dots pictures she liked to do. In a way, it was similar, since a kind of *picture* would come out of the chart, too.

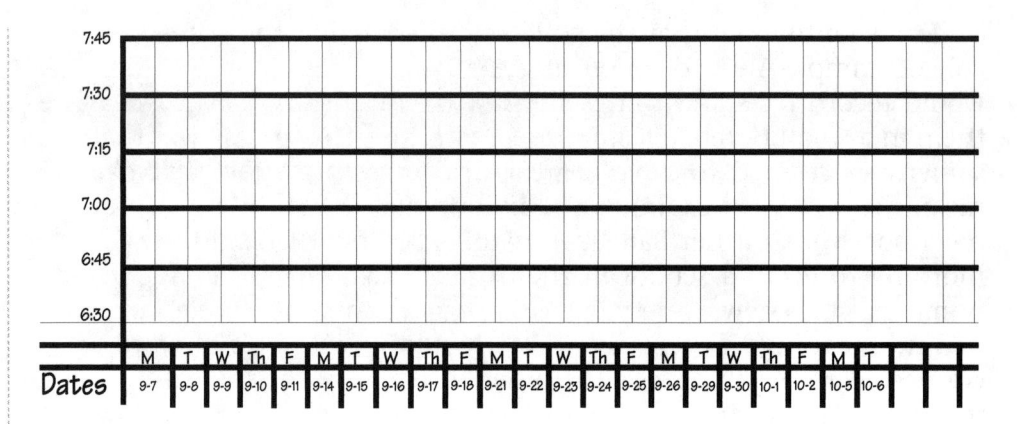

FIGURE 9.1 Erin's empty line graph

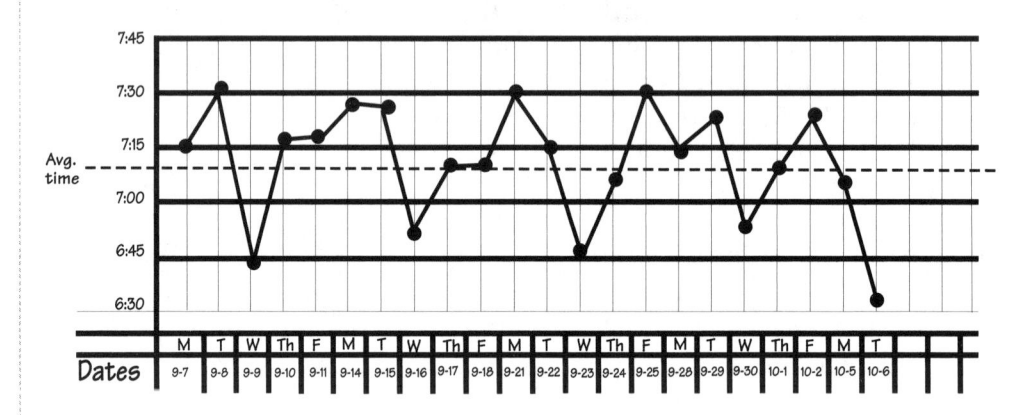

FIGURE 9.2 Mr. Badgekar's departure times

The chart was full. Erin had collected enough data to show a whole month. She had learned that there had to be enough data points to see patterns. Just one or two points would not tell her anything. She also knew that each point needed to show numbers with something in common. What they had in common was Mr. Badgekar's school week schedule. It would not make sense to include Labor Day, for example. He did not leave for school that day but instead went to the beach with his family.

Each day's time had been recorded. Now Erin was able to look at the chart to try to figure out what it showed. Figure 9.2 shows what she saw.

She could see that at least once each week, Mr. Badgekar left earlier than on the other days. She decided to ask him about this pattern. Of course, she knew she needed to be tactful about this. She did not want him to think she had been spying on him. Of course, that was exactly what she had been doing.

Erin told Mr. Badgekar that she was learning how to keep charts that could provide information. She confessed that she had practiced by collecting data about the times he left for school. He was interested in her study, since he used line graphs to keep track of the average grades of his own class on weekly tests.

"You're right about the way I leave early some days," he said. "And you'll see that the early days are always Wednesdays. That's the day I have breakfast with my team teachers." Erin was delighted when she heard that, since it gave meaning to what had been only a number in her list of data.

"What other information does the chart show?" Mr. Badgekar asked. The two of them looked closely. On October 6, it showed a much earlier departure time. Erin asked about that. Mr. Badgekar had left his driveway at 6:30 A.M. that day. Erin heard his garage door shut and his car pull out of the driveway. She had jumped out of bed in order to jot down the information, so now she remembered it clearly. "I left early to play racquetball with a friend," he laughed. "You don't miss anything!" He asked her to tell him the average time he had left for school. Erin figured the average by adding all the times, and then dividing by the number of days. The average time was 7:08 A.M. She drew a dotted line to show this on the chart.

The chart was interesting, and it helped Erin to understand how line graphs can provide information. She had learned how to collect data and analyze it. Now she felt she could tackle many other issues and analyze them with line graphs.

Erin decided to keep track of her own piano practice records. "I guess I need to look at myself rather than my neighbor, if I want to do something useful," she sighed. Her piano teacher had asked her to write down the amount of time that she practiced each day. Erin had been a

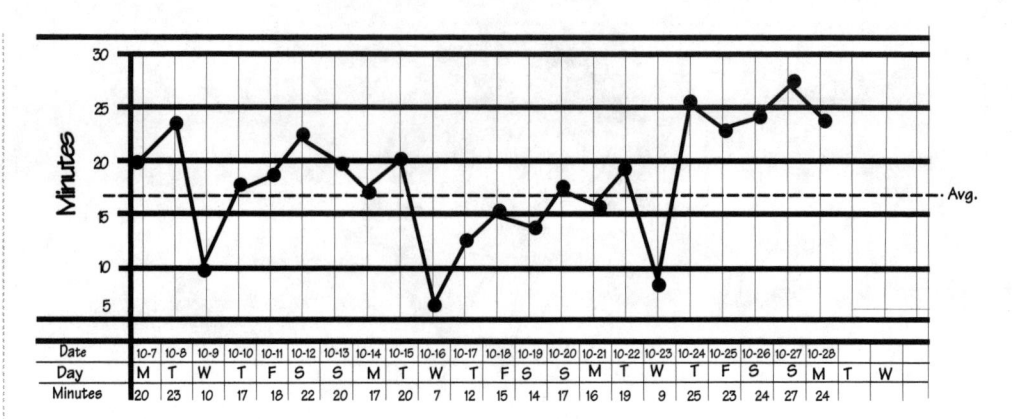

FIGURE 9.3 Erin's piano practice record

little sloppy with those records. She often forgot to write down her practice times until the day she was scheduled for her lesson. She could not always count on her memory to be correct.

Making another chart, Erin told her piano teacher what she was doing and how she would use the information. She asked Mrs. Hess if she could keep track for a month before talking it over with her. Erin's teacher thought that would be fine, especially since, if it worked, it might be a method that would help her other piano students. After a month, Erin looked at her chart (see Figure 9.3).

Erin was surprised to see how much the lines went up and down. She thought that she practiced regularly. Now she saw that even though she had regular practice sessions, some were long and some were very short. Erin could see how the numbers for her practice times were changed into information just by keeping track and making her chart. She figured that her average practice time was 17 minutes—not nearly enough to improve.

Without the chart, her practice times were just numbers. Or, as Mr. Badgekar pointed out to her, they were like the scores of football games without the names of the teams: 14–0, 7–21, 8–16, 10–3. It would be frustrating to know only the score of a game without knowing the teams. The numbers by themselves had no meaning.

The chart left Erin with some questions. It also made her wonder about the reasons that she had practiced longer on some days and hardly at all on others. She decided to keep notes about her practices. Later, she used a Pareto chart (chapter 10). She discovered that Wednesdays seemed to be the days that she practiced least. Finally, she asked herself why this was the case, and did a fishbone diagram to help answer the mystery of why. That's another story, but perhaps you can guess at some of her reasons, and make your own fishbone diagram about the main cause for poor practices on Wednesday. (Hint: Her lessons were always on Tuesdays.)

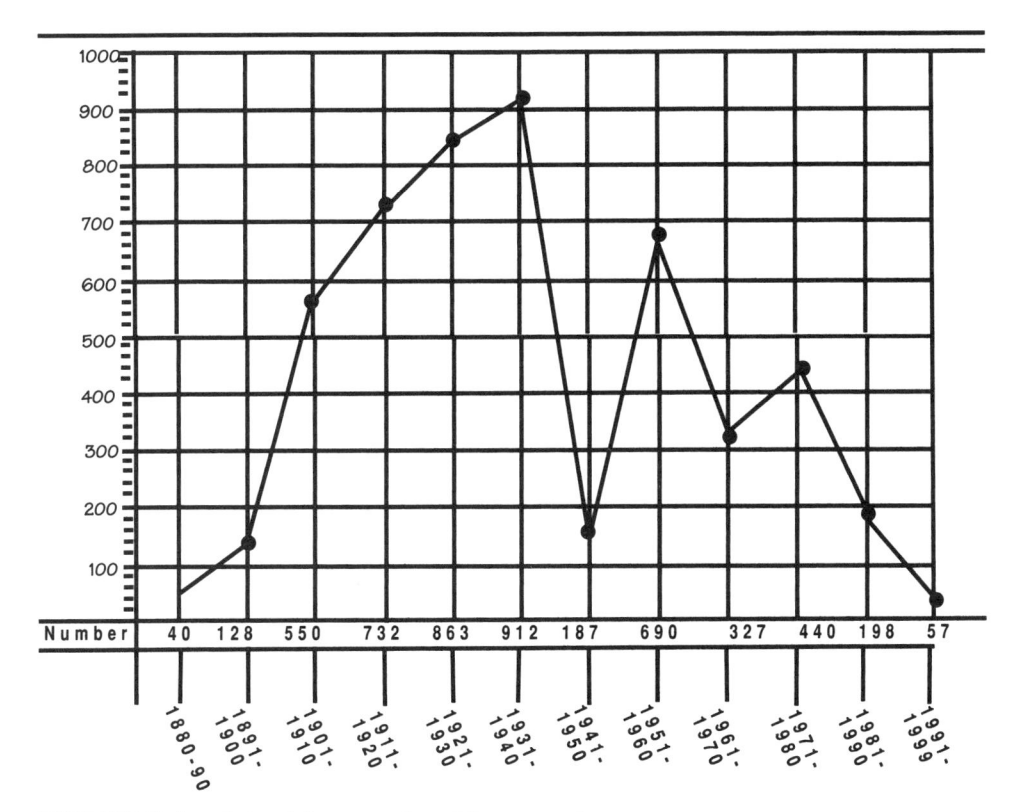

FIGURE 9.4 Ariyah's pennies: Line graph

You will remember Ariyah and his pennies from the last chapter. He counted the money in everyone's coin collections. In addition, he was interested in how old the pennies were. When he used the muffin tins for Mrs. Levy's penny collection, he labelled the cups by date. If Ariyah made a line graph for the pennies in Mrs. Levy's bank, it might look like the one in Figure 9.4. The patterns that you see on this chart may make you ask some new questions. What questions do you have, based on the line graph above?

You can see that two different tools—histograms and line graphs—can give different information about the same data. You might want to try using different tools on the same data as you work your way through this book.

SUGGESTIONS FOR USING LINE GRAPHS

- Gather your data (numbers) before making the actual chart. This will help you decide what numbers to use on the left side of the chart.
- Collect data on check sheets first, leaving space for comments or notes. Then transfer the numbers to the line graph.
- Be sure that you have enough data to analyze.

- Line graphs show data collected *in time order.* This means in the order that it happens. An example would be Monday, Tuesday, Wednesday, or times that follow each other (8:00, 9:00, 10:00), or consecutive months (December, January, February). This order needs to be kept in order to see trends and patterns.
- If you want to figure your average, add up all the data points, then divide by the number of data points.

OTHER TOOLS YOU MAY USE WITH LINE GRAPHS

- Check sheets, to help collect and record data

- Pareto diagrams, to see the frequency of the occurrences and to narrow the scope of the analysis

- Fishbone diagrams, to organize reasons for the patterns that you may see on your line graph

- Lotus flower diagrams, to develop ideas for specific problems for which you might want to create charts

NAME: _____

CLASS: _____

DATE: _____

MY OWN THINKING TOOLS PAGE
LINE GRAPHS

First, Some Practice

You will have practice in *collecting* data when you make a line graph on your own. For practice in *recording* data on a line graph, use the numbers listed on the check sheet below, and write them on the line graph at the end of this chapter. (Or ask your teacher to make a copy of that line graph for you to use.)

Data: Library books checked out from the school library.

Monday, February 20:	30
Tuesday, February 21:	42
Wednesday, February 22:	53
Thursday, February 23:	39
Friday, February 24:	60
Monday, February 27:	12
Tuesday, February 28:	68
Wednesday, March 1:	43
Thursday, March 2:	49
Friday, March 3:	64
Monday, March 6:	20
Tuesday, March 7:	57
Wednesday, March 8:	54
Thursday, March 9:	67
Friday, March 10:	75

Line Graph for Library Books

The scale of numbers on the left is for how many books are checked out. In Figure 9.3, these numbers stood for the number of minutes Erin practiced. The dates are on the bottom of the chart. Find the number for each day, and put a dot on your line graph that corresponds to the date. You may not see the exact number on the lefthand scale. For example, you may not find "62" on the left, but only lines that show "60" and "65." Try to guess where 62 will fall between those two lines, and put your dot there. To make a scale for the left side, follow the rule in the Glossary. The reason for the rule is to be sure that there is enough room on the chart for all of your data points.

After you have made dots for all the numbers, connect the dots in order. Is your line straight, or does it go up and down a lot? Overall, does it go gradually up or down during the three-week period? What days have the lowest number of books checked out? Do you see any other patterns? With a partner, look at your charts, and describe the patterns that you see.

_____

_____

_____

_____

_____

_____

Other sources of data that may have already been collected in your school include the following:

- Substitute teachers in your building each day
- Absences reported to the office each day
- Meals served in the cafeteria
- Copies made by the copy machine each day
- Enrollment in the school for the past 15 or 20 years
- Cars entering the school grounds each morning to drop off students

Using any of these sources of data, you can practice making run charts. Then you can study the chart to gather more information about the data that you have recorded.

Now It's Your Turn...

Now that you have made a chart using data that someone else has collected, it's time for you to collect data for yourself. You can do this either alone or with a partner or group. For groups, form teams of 3 or 4 students, and decide what information you would like to have. Then collect data that will help give that information. Some examples are the following:

1. Keep track of your own scores on weekly spelling tests or other regular quizzes. You may already have some of these scores, or your teacher will have a record of them. If they have dates on them, you can use the ones you already have to create a line graph. Chart the number of correct responses for your entire group on these weekly tests.

2. With a partner, select winning football teams before each series of weekend games. Record the number you got right the first week, the second week, the third week, and so on.

3. If you play on an athletic team, record statistics about your own team, such as the number of goals scored, fouls against your team, corner kicks (for soccer), free throws (basketball), runs batted in (baseball), strikes (bowling), accurate serves (tennis), etc.

4. Keep a check sheet of the number of times you fall as you learn to ride a bike or roller blade. Write the data on a line graph. (Here's your chance to go out and play, as part of doing your homework!)

5. Record the number of students who bring their lunches from home each day, or the number who have fresh fruit for lunch.

6. Record the times that students in physical education class can run 50 yards. Use a stop watch and write the number on a check sheet before you make a line graph.

7. In your writing portfolio, count the number of new words that you have used each week in your papers.

8. If you are learning keyboarding skills on the computer, you can keep data about the words per minute that you type each week.

After you have picked one of the topics from the list above (or one of your own choosing), write the data on a *check sheet*. (Make a copy of the blank check sheet in chapter 6 or use a ruler to make your own version.) This is the best way to start collecting data. Later, you will make your line graph using this data.

Label the chart and put in words that show what the data refer to. For example, if you are using the football team data, write "Team" and "Scores" across the top of your chart. Then record the weekly games in the lefthand column. Write the game scores for each game in the space to the right.

Now you're ready to put this data on a line graph. Write the topic for your line graph at the top of the chart. Copy the blank line graph that you will find at the end of this chapter or use the one below.

On the lefthand side of your chart, write the scale for your data. Your teacher will help you decide how to scale your chart and what to write across the bottom of the chart as well. Record your data by using dots at the place where the date and bus time cross. Then connect these dots, using a small ruler to be sure they are straight.

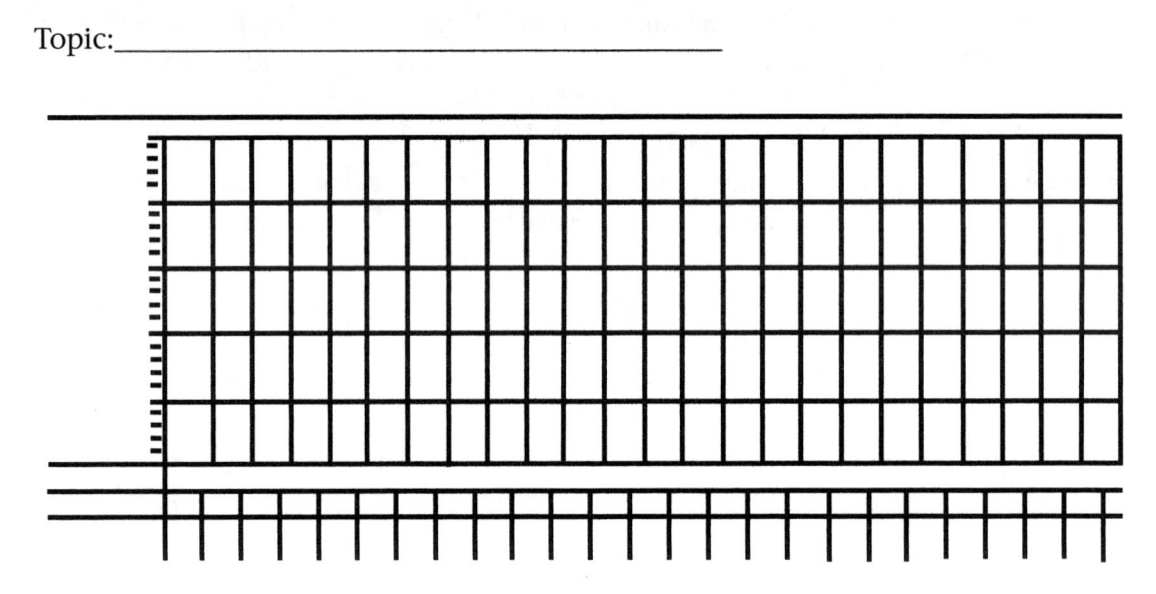

Topic:_____

Look at what you have drawn. When you look at your chart, you have a kind of *picture* of whatever you are charting. You've connected the dots to show the pattern. You may be able to see that the bus is often late on Monday afternoons, for example. You can also see the average time that the bus arrives. This information may make you ask "Why?" What trends do you see in the data you have just charted? What questions do you have about the chart and what it shows? Write three good *why?* questions here:

1._____

2._____

3._____

Reminder: For all the charts you make, you can use the blank line graph on the last page of this chapter. You can make as many copies of this as you need for practice.

HOME CONNECTION

You may want to ask someone in your family to be your partner. You can teach your parents or brother or sister how to do line graphs while you practice. Choose one of the following sources of data, or think of one that you would prefer to track.

1. Check the thermostat in your home and write down the temperature that it shows. Write the temperature on a check sheet. Be sure that you have also written the date and time.

    Check the thermostat again at regular times throughout the day or week, making sure that you are collecting data at regular intervals of time. These could be every hour, once each day, once each morning and once each afternoon for two weeks, etc.

2. Dentists say you should brush your teeth for at least two minutes each time you brush. Using a clock with a second hand, keep track of the number of seconds you are actually brushing each time.

3. If you fish regularly, record the number of trout that you throw back—or the ones you catch—each time you go fishing. Compare your run chart with your fishing partners (your parents or brothers or sisters, for example).

4. Another healthy practice: Doctors say that everyone should drink at least eight glasses of water every day. Keep a check sheet to record the amount of water you drink.

5. Keep track of the number of minutes you watch television at home. Record the times over a period of a month, and see if you can identify any patterns, either for yourself or for your family.

6. Count the number of red (or blue or yellow) cars you see as you ride to school each day. If you go on a family vacation, count the cars that you see for each hour on your trip.

NAME: _____

CLASS: _____

DATE: _____

LINE GRAPH TEMPLATE

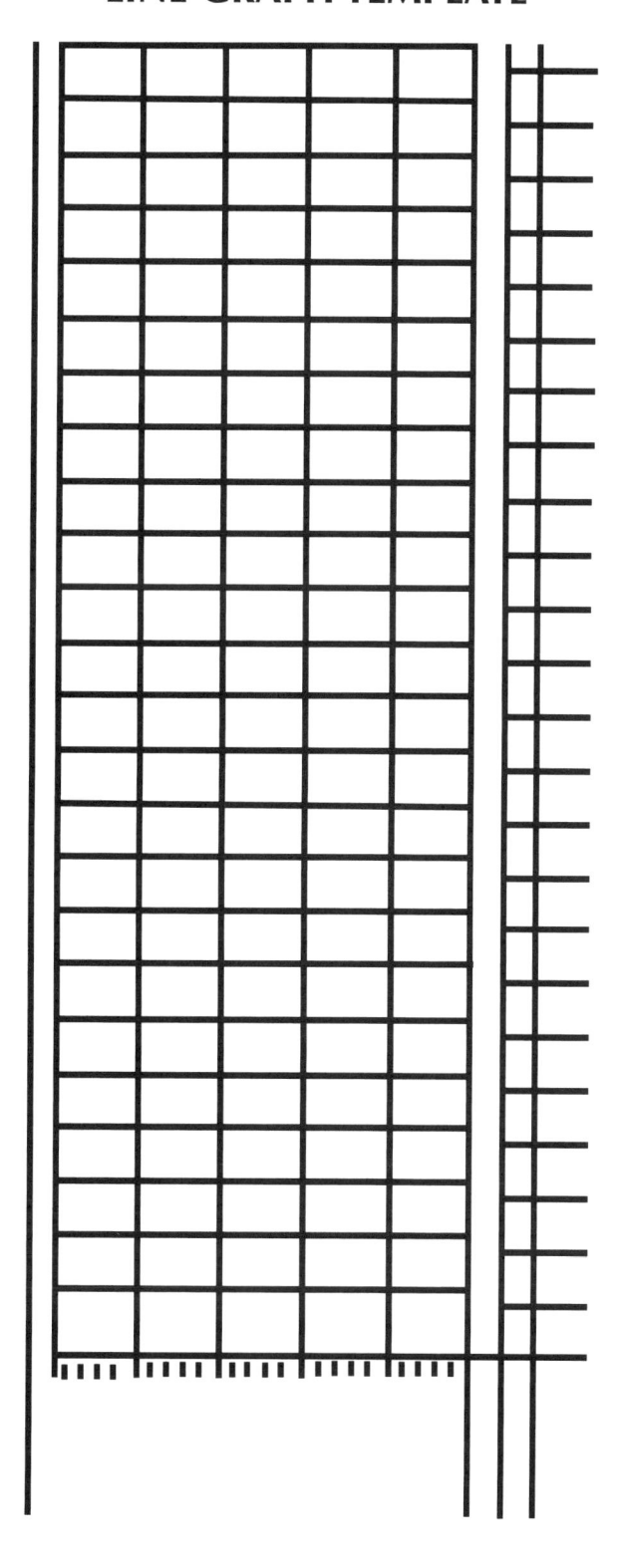

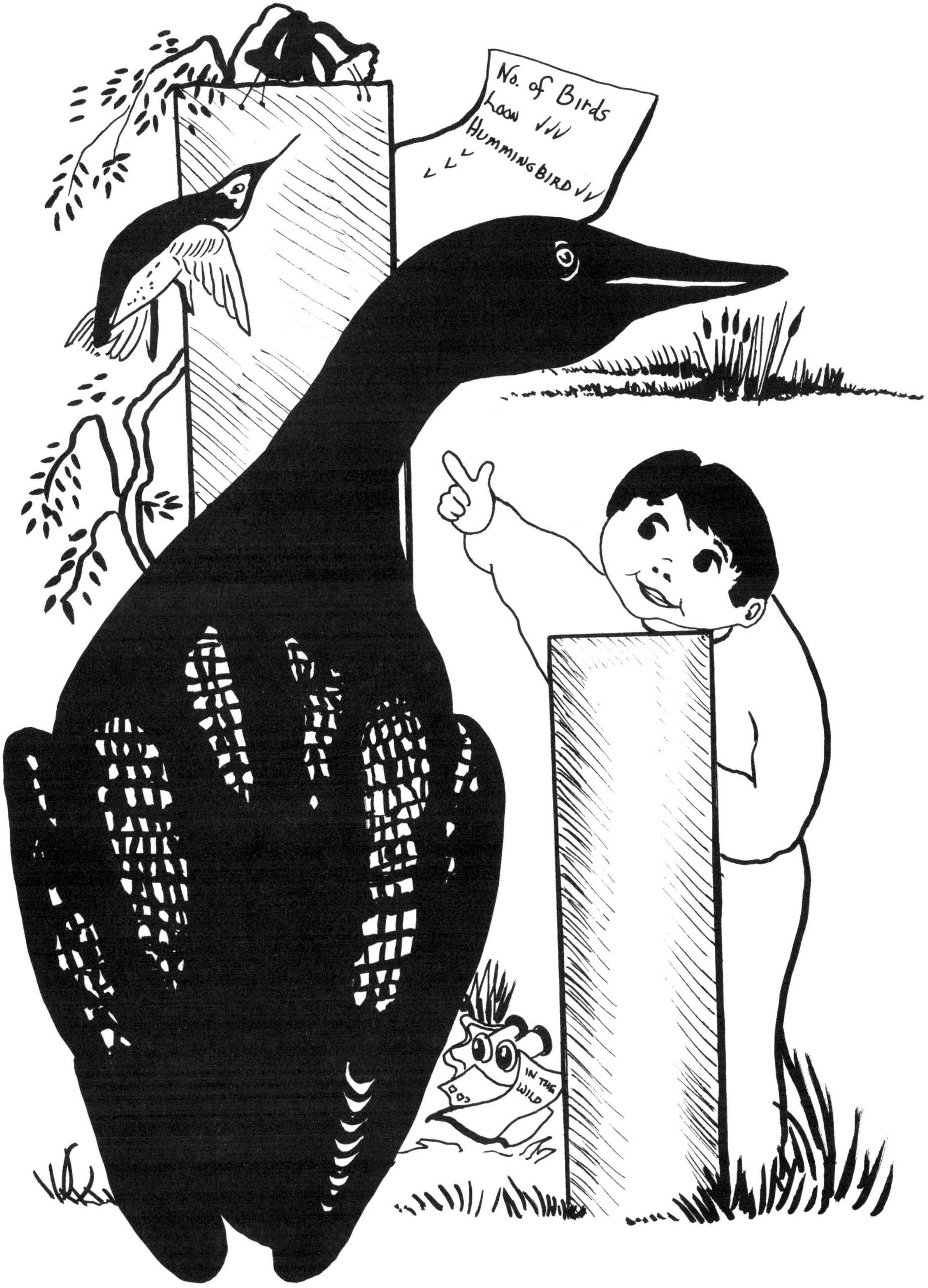
No. of Birds
Loon ✓✓✓
HUMMINGBIRD ✓✓ ✓✓✓
IN THE WILD

CHAPTER 10

PARETO DIAGRAMS
Finding the Biggest Group

Chris thought of himself as a kind of collector. He *collected* birds; that is, he kept track of birds that he saw around his home in Vermont. He also kept track when he visited his grandmother on the seacoast or his aunt and uncle in the Midwest. He had other friends who collected shells, rocks, and leaves. He found that he had lots in common with them. Anyone who collects something needs to figure out how to classify whatever is in the collection. Chris also needed to keep records of when and where he saw each one.

Chris had a very old copy of Peterson's *Field Guide to the Birds* that his grandmother had given to him. He sometimes read other sources at the library as well. He was surprised by the author's comments in the preface of his book. Mr. Peterson said he often received letters from readers. They sometimes made suggestions for his next book. Some of the suggestions had to do with *nomenclature,* or what birds are called. Chris could see differences in the names of birds between his old book and later editions in the library.

The author said he had more than a thousand filing cards with ideas about the newest edition of his book. Chris could imagine the confusion of trying to group that many different things. He was trying to classify his own small number of sightings of common birds. He felt he needed a system that would fit the official bird classification system but would also be useful for his own experience.

Peterson, the author of the bird book, told his readers to make the guide a personal thing. He said that he had seen copies torn apart, shifted around, and then bound again to suit the owner's taste. Chris was encouraged. Of course, he had no intention of ripping the book apart. But he now felt that he could come up with his own system of classifying birds. What he really wanted was a way to translate what he had in his notebooks to some kind of chart. He thought this would tell the story of his bird watching better than words in a notebook.

Chris decided to begin by making a *Pareto diagram* to help identify the kinds of birds he had seen most frequently in his sightings.

First, he used a check sheet, writing the names of the birds and the number of sightings for each bird (Figure 10.1). In his notebook, he had written down much more than this. He had included the time of day, the place, the sex of the bird, its song, and other important data about each sighting. But it was hard to tell from the notebook which birds he had seen most frequently. A Pareto diagram would give this information at a glance.

144 CHAPTER 10

Hummingbirds	𝍷𝍷𝍷 𝍷𝍷𝍷 𝍷𝍷𝍷
Loons	I
Thrushes	IIII
Finches	𝍷𝍷𝍷 𝍷𝍷𝍷 𝍷𝍷𝍷 𝍷𝍷𝍷 𝍷𝍷𝍷 I
Pigeons	𝍷𝍷𝍷 𝍷𝍷𝍷 III
Cardinals	𝍷𝍷𝍷 𝍷𝍷𝍷
Buntings	II
Juncos	III
Sparrows	𝍷𝍷𝍷 𝍷𝍷𝍷 𝍷𝍷𝍷 𝍷𝍷𝍷 𝍷𝍷𝍷 IIII
Robins	𝍷𝍷𝍷 𝍷𝍷𝍷 𝍷𝍷𝍷 II
Grackles	𝍷𝍷𝍷 𝍷𝍷𝍷 𝍷𝍷𝍷
Owls	I
Terns	II
Merganzers	
Geese	𝍷𝍷𝍷 III

FIGURE 10.1 Bird sightings: Check sheet

Chris knew that his classifications were not as exact as those in the book. For example, a cardinal is actually a kind of finch, according to his old bird book. Finches were only one kind of bird, it said. But he often saw gold finches or purple finches. He wanted to keep these separate for his own purposes.

When he looked at the chart, he realized that hummingbirds were among the groups of birds he had seen most often. It was in the top four or five, in fact. This was hard to figure out, since they were among the most unusual birds in his area.

"Of course," he pointed out to his grandmother. "It's because you have a hummingbird feeder right outside the kitchen window, and I see them all the time." Others, like the owl and loons, were birds that had not come to feeders but had been spotted in the wild.

Chris decided to create a *Pareto diagram* for the birds that visited feeders in his yard or at other places he visited. First, he counted the number of sightings that he had recorded on his check sheet. To make a Pareto diagram, he drew two lines that were at a right angle to each other, like a fence is to the ground next to it. Along the upright line (the fence), he made a scale that showed the numbers of sightings he had. At the top was the total number of sightings.

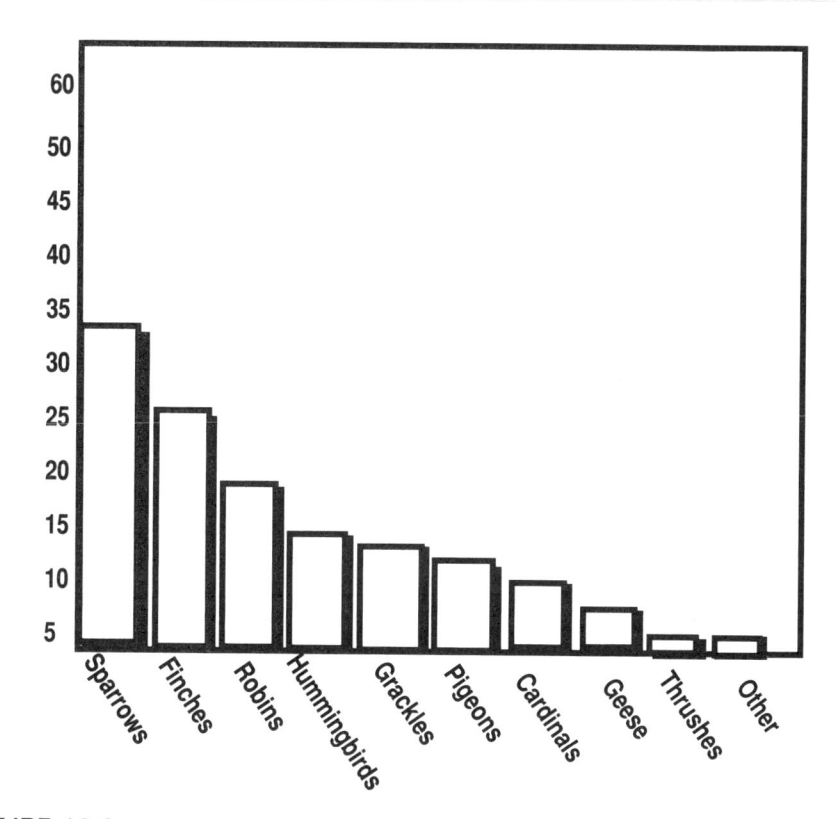

FIGURE 10.2 Bird sightings: Pareto diagram

Along the horizontal line (the ground), he would write the names of each category or kind of bird that he had seen. The largest category would come first, down to the smallest category way over on the right side of his chart. His check sheet helped him to know the size of each category.

Then he created bars for each of these groups. Since several categories had only one or two entries, he put these together and labelled that bar *other*. Figure 10.2 reflects Chris's completed Pareto diagram.

He knew that if someone asked him about birds that he saw, he would be able to report the kind of birds that he had seen most often. He could even show someone the Pareto diagram. It showed the numbers of birds he had seen in all of his sightings, regardless of location.

Chris realized that he could make other Pareto diagrams as well. Each different kind would give different information. Figure 10.2 reflects all the birds. Chris could also make Pareto diagrams for the following:

- Only the kinds of finches he had seen
- Only the birds he had seen in their natural habitats
- Number of birds seen, by time of day
- Only the birds in Vermont (Figure 10.3)
- Only seacoast bird sightings

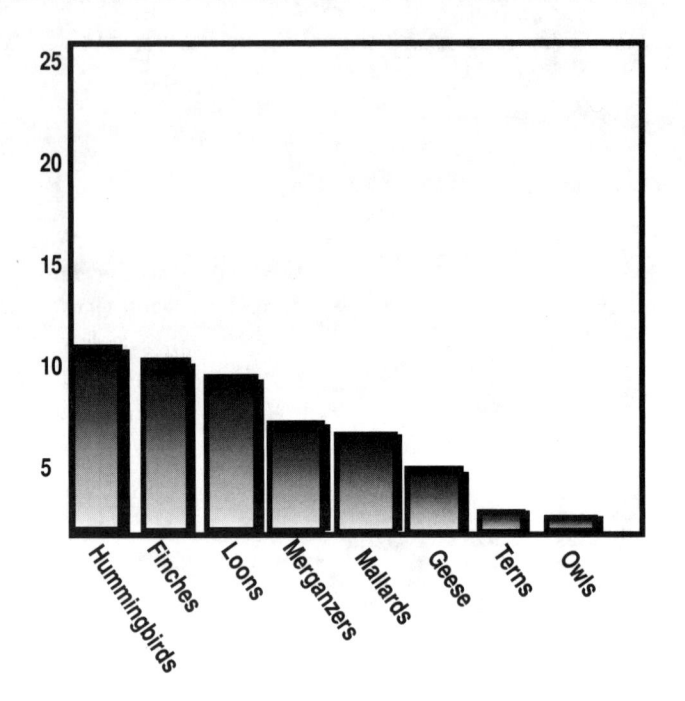

FIGURE 10.3 Birds seen in Vermont: Pareto diagram

Any of these Pareto diagrams would help Chris see the greatest number in each analysis. He also began to understand that sometimes what seems to be the most frequent sighting is not necessarily the one with the greatest interest. Seeing and hearing a loon at the lake in Vermont, for example, far surpassed the excitement of watching sparrows at his father's bird feeder. But there were only a few loons in his overall data, while there were dozens of sparrows.

Then he made several different Pareto diagrams, one showing the birds that he had observed only in the morning. Others showed the birds that he had seen in the wild, birds that were native to Vermont, and several other kinds of sightings. Each diagram told a slightly different story. Chris realized that there are many different ways to look at the same numbers. With each different chart, he was able to learn something new about his bird sightings.

SUGGESTIONS FOR USING PARETO DIAGRAMS

- As you collect your data, gather more information than you think you will need. This will give you more choices about what you want to use for your charts.
- Remember that Pareto diagrams help you to discover which of your categories have the biggest number. They do not tell you which ones are most important. For example, a Pareto diagram can tell what kind of injuries take place most frequently on the playground, but it will not tell you that a broken leg is far more serious than a scraped knee.
- Color the bars on your Pareto diagram so they will be different from one another.

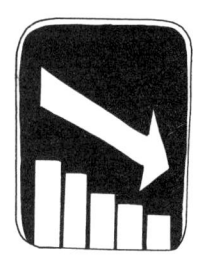

OTHER TOOLS YOU MAY USE WITH PARETO DIAGRAMS

- Check sheets, to collect numbers of occurrences

- Line graphs, to reflect the number of birds seen over a period of time

- Fishbone diagrams, to help identify root causes for a specific category's frequency

NAME: _____

CLASS: _____

DATE: _____

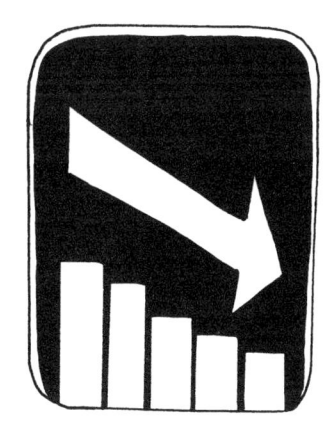

MY OWN THINKING TOOLS PAGE
PARETO DIAGRAMS

First, Some Practice

Using packages of chocolate candies with different colors, separate the candies into piles of different colors: red, brown, yellow, orange, blue. Without eating *any* of the candies, arrange them on a napkin in front of you so that the biggest group is furthest to the left, the next largest number next, and so on. What you see is a Pareto diagram. It does not have labels for the numbers or names of each color, but it still looks like a Pareto diagram. If you were to transfer this edible Pareto to paper, it might look like Figure 10.4.

You may want to color the stacks of candies to correspond with their names. Make your own Pareto diagram from the package of candies you have opened. Are yours similar to Figure 10.4? What is the total number of candies in your package? Check to see if your classmates all have the same number in their packages. Now compare the mixtures of colors. You are probably seeing variation among the packages. If you want to make a line graph that shows this variation, use the same package of candies to practice that tool as well. But first, make your Pareto diagram. You can do that in the space provided on the next page.

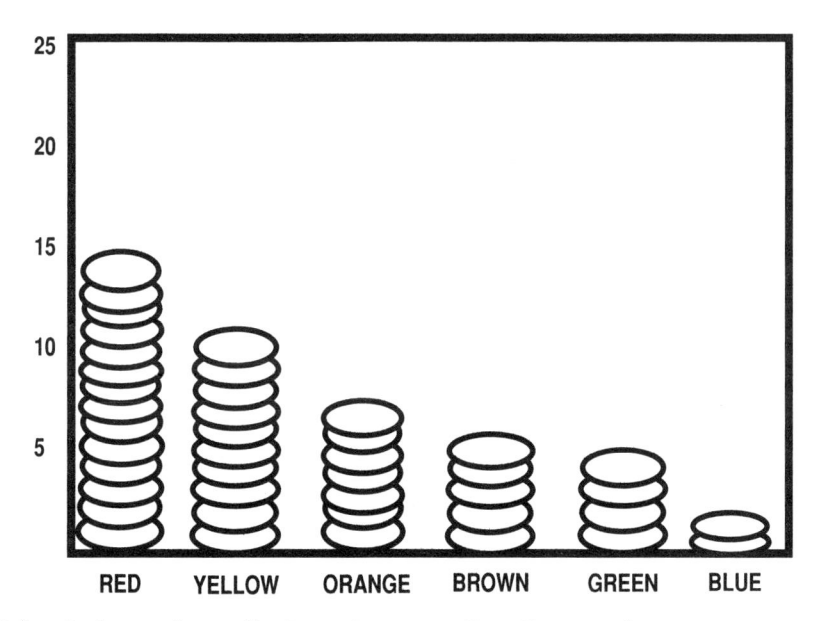

FIGURE 10.4 Colors of small chocolate candies: Pareto diagram

My Pareto diagram title:_____Date_____

In this case, all the different colors are right there for you to count. Sometimes you will need to gather information instead of having it collected in a bag or box like the candies. You can use a check sheet to record your data. Another way to get information is to write questions and conduct a survey. By writing your questions down, you can be sure that you have asked everyone for the same information.

To make other Pareto diagrams, use a copy of the blank chart at the end of this chapter. Write the names of the groups at the bottom (after you have counted them), and the scale along the left side.

As a class, use a large container of crayons if you have one in your classroom. Separate these by color and create a Pareto diagram from that data. First, separate the crayons by color. Next, count each color and write the number on a check sheet. Add up all the crayons to get the total number that was in the box. Then you can write numbers on the left side of your chart.

Across the bottom, write the names of the colors, with the biggest pile first, the second biggest next, and so on. Now you can make bars that go as high as the number in each group. If there are 23 red crayons, for example, draw the bar so the top of it is equal to where 23 might be on your chart. Twenty-three may be between 20 and 25, if you have marked your tall line in steps of 5, for example. Your Pareto chart might look similar to Figure 10.5.

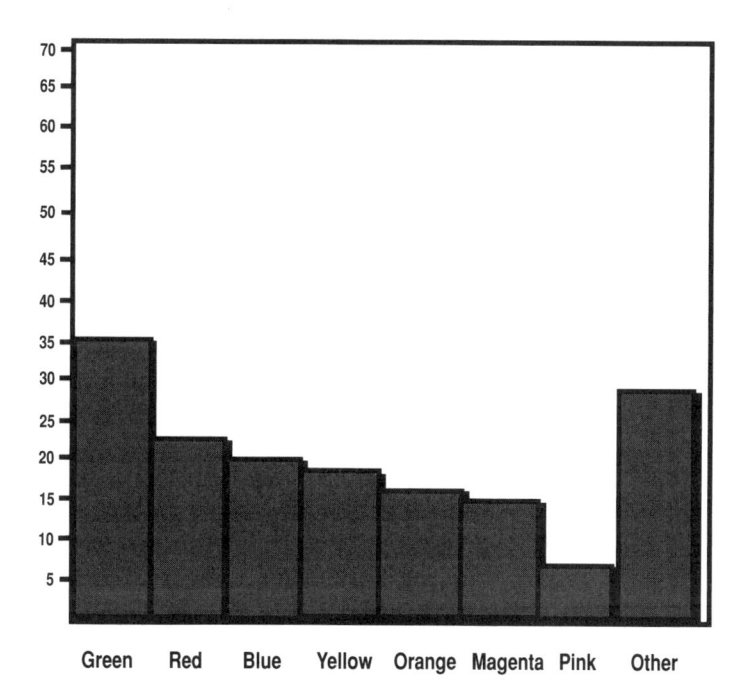

FIGURE 10.5 Colors of crayons in box

Now, It's Your Turn...

If it is autumn, you can use the fall leaves to develop a Pareto diagram. Rake up a pile of leaves from the trees at your school, park, or home or other places where you can rake leaves. (This might be your opportunity to do a good deed for your neighbor!) Bring a small bag of the leaves to school and, with a partner, identify them.

After you have identified the leaves, organize them into groups that each show one kind of tree: maple, hickory, and so on. Which pile has the greatest number? You can make a Pareto diagram from the data that you collected with your rake. Count all the leaves first, so you will know how to make a scale for the left side. Then count each group. Make a Pareto diagram by drawing bars that show the kind with the greatest number, then the next, and so on. Be creative—your bars might be piles of leaves rather than simple line bars. Use the blank chart at the end of this chapter or a sheet of construction paper for your chart. Your bars might be created by cutting different colors of construction paper and pasting them in the right places.

Another project can be based on a simple survey. With a partner, ask all your classmates what kinds of books they used for book reports (mysteries, historical novels, poetry, adventure, fantasy, etc.). Make a Pareto diagram that reflects the number in each group.

Use Pareto diagrams to keep track of your own learning, too. For example, if you are practicing your multiplication facts, notice the number of combinations that you know without hesitation. Keep track of how many 7s you know (7 × 3, 7 × 4, 7 × 5, etc.). Which of the number combinations do you know best? A Pareto diagram can help you see this. Numbers along the bottom (1s, 2s, 3s, 4s, 5s, 6s, etc.) will show where your strengths are. The first bar will indicate the combinations that

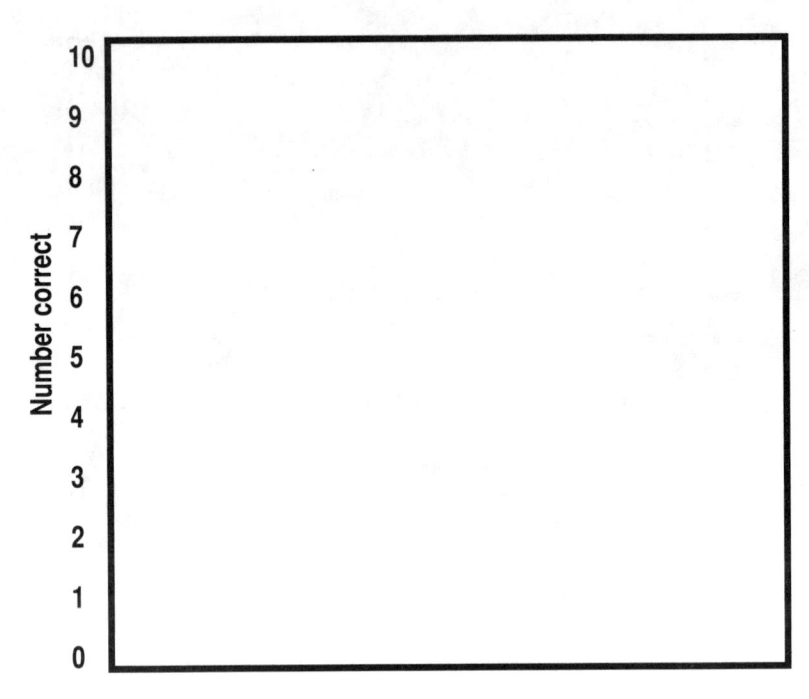

[Empty graph with y-axis labeled "Number correct" from 0 to 10]

FIGURE 10.6 Multiplication facts: Pareto diagram

you most frequently have correct. Figure 10.6 shows how this Pareto diagram can be set up. Fill in the right numbers for your own multiplication facts. Arrange the combinations in the order to show the ones you know best down to the ones you seem to know least. Combinations might be 1s, 2s, 3s, 4s, 5s, 6s, 7s, 8s, 9s, and 10s, for example.

Question: How is this different from a histogram? What would you need to know in order to use your Pareto data for a histogram? (Remember, histogram data are arranged along a continuous line, or *continuum*.) Write your answer here:

_____
_____

Here are a few other ideas for collecting data for Pareto diagrams. Add some of your own ideas to this list.

1. The states (or countries) that your classmates have visited
2. Neighborhoods where students live
3. Musical instruments that students play
4. Preferred athletic activities among your classmates
5. _____
6. _____
7. _____

HOME CONNECTION

Remember that a Pareto diagram helps to identify which group is the largest. With your family, select something where finding the largest group is important. For example, who gets the most mail each day? (This might lead to a discussion about whose job it should be to get the mail from the mailbox.) Who drinks the most milk?

Pareto analysis helps you think about how things are classified. Sometimes this data is useful in solving a problem. Other times, it's just interesting. Here are some possibilities for you to practice Pareto diagrams at home. Add your own ideas to the list.

1. Colors (or models) of the cars that go by your house during a certain period of time
2. Kinds of pets in your neighborhood
3. Toys that kids in your neighborhood or class like best
4. Magazines that people in your family or neighborhood read
5. Favorite movies or books
6. People's favorite foods or kinds of food (for example, what is your favorite kind of pizza?)
7. Where the people you know spend their vacations
8. _____
9. _____
10. _____

NAME: _____

CLASS: _____

DATE: _____

PARETO DIAGRAM TEMPLATE

Title _____

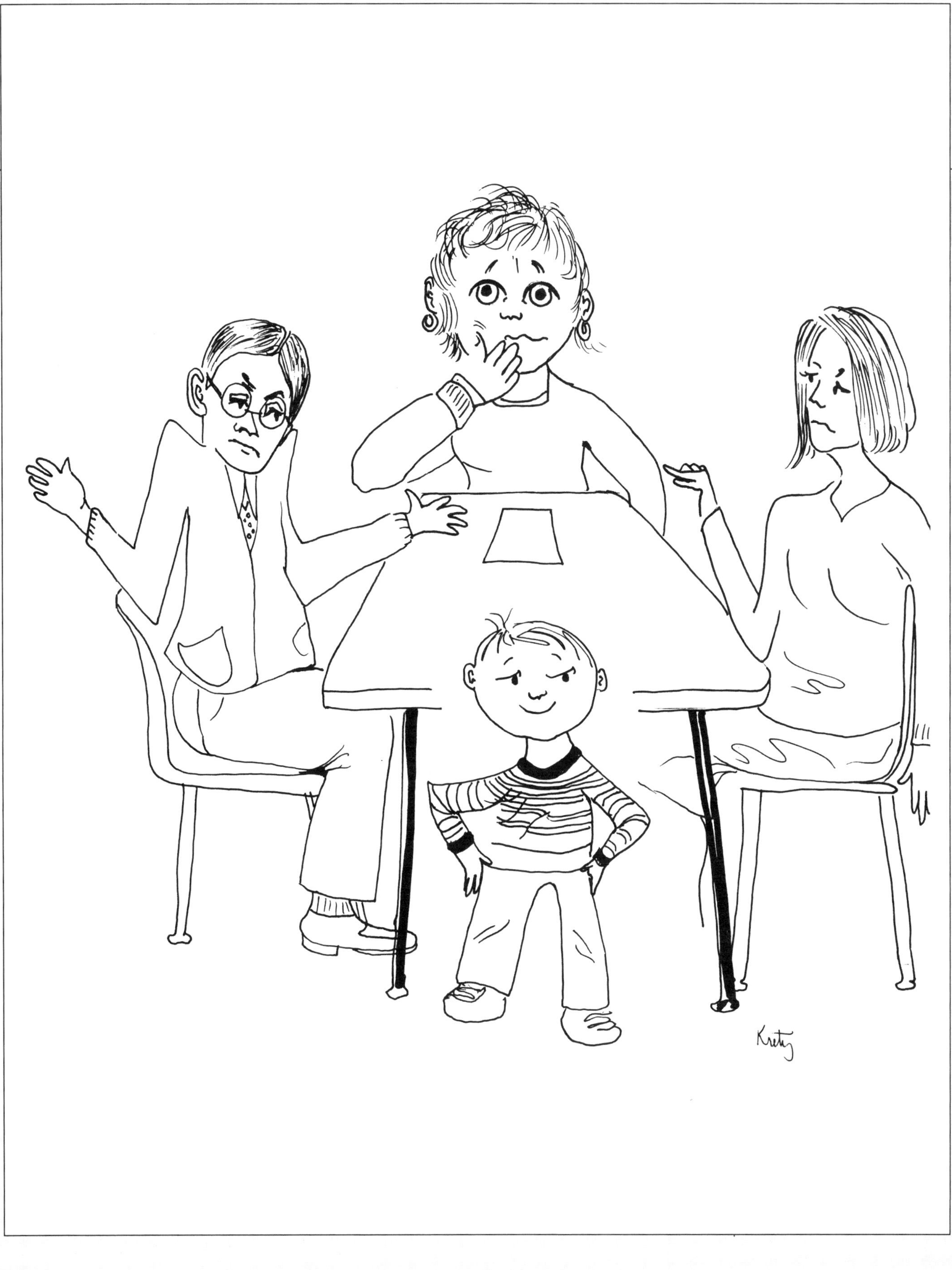

CHAPTER 11

PUTTING IT ALL TOGETHER
Data Folders and Data Centers

Miss Walker was not looking forward to the parent-student-teacher conference that had been scheduled with Victor's mother and father. There had been an apparent lack of communication between the school and the home in Victor's case, and Miss Walker dreaded a confrontation with the parents over his progress in her fourth grade classroom.

As she reviewed her grade book, she saw that Victor's homework had often been submitted late and that penalties had ensued for nearly every assignment. A major writing assignment had never been handed in, and she had written "messy" in her grade book next to the entry for a math paper. Victor, on the other hand, had told his parents that he was doing very well in school. Miss Walker knew that he was headed for an unsatisfactory grade at the conclusion of the marking period—and that *she* was headed for an explanation for his poor performance this term.

Sure enough, when Mr. and Mrs. Fostwick arrived for their conference, tension emerged in spite of Miss Walker's best efforts to be positive. "Victor plays well with others in gym class," she said, but as she looked at his grades for the term, she found little else about which to comment positively. When she shared his grades with them, the Fostwicks became defensive. This was the first they had heard that Victor's performance was less than perfect.

They turned their attention to Victor. "Miss Walker says you didn't do your homework assignments when you were supposed to," they said.

"Yes, I did," he responded innocently. "She must have lost them." Miss Walker found herself in a "she-said-he-said" confrontation with Victor, whose parents clearly believed their child.

The conference went from bad to worse, as Victor looked wide-eyed at his parents, and his parents looked accusingly at Miss Walker. The teacher had ample evidence of his grades throughout the term, but these were posted in her grade book. The only examples of his work that she was able to show Victor's parents were the art projects that had been posted on the bulletin board in the classroom and were now in his art portfolio.

After the Fostwicks had left the conference, Miss Walker turned to Mrs. Cummings, an experienced teacher, for advice about how to handle a situation such as Victor's. "What can I do to keep this kind of conference from happening again?" she pleaded.

"Have you thought about ways to enlist the support of the parents in your work with Victor?" Mrs. Cummings probed gently.

"Support? They don't really want to support me; they think their child is perfect, and I'm just getting in the way," Miss Walker responded.

"Well, then, let's think of ways to bolster your case when you meet them again. Do you have any of Victor's homework assignments?" Miss Walker shook her head. She had little evidence that Victor was even in the class, apart from her own records in the grade book.

"Then let's start with that. You keep an art portfolio—how about a daily work portfolio? Keep all of Victor's work, just to show the quality that it evinces. That's the first thing," Mrs. Cummings said.

"I'd have to do that for all the students in my class, I guess," Miss Walker said somewhat doubtfully. "That sounds like a lot of work."

"Well, the trick is to have Victor and your other students keep their own portfolios, not to create more work for you. You can give them lists of what should be included, and they can check those off as they put their papers inside."

Miss Walker knew about check sheets. She had used them to record who had brought lunch money each week. She began to envision the ways in which she could help her students use check sheets to keep the work current in their portfolios. She began to make a list of items that students could collect for their portfolios.

- Spelling words from list #1
- Spelling words from list #2
- Spelling words from list #3
- Writing about Halloween
- Math homework or "Mad Minutes" scores
- Multiplication facts

Recalling the conference with Victor and his parents, she knew that having the work might help them to see how well he was doing with assignments. Because it would not give clues about homework submitted late or provide any indication of real progress over time, she devised a second check sheet, this time for the entire class, to record on-time submissions. Each time a paper or other assignment was submitted on time, the student would be encouraged to paste a sticker into the square representing that assignment. For assignments submitted late, the square would remain blank. In addition, Miss Walker would stamp a date on each assignment as it was submitted for evaluation or feedback.

"It's just like an art portfolio," she commented.

"Yes, and that is helpful," replied Mrs. Cummings. "But let's take this to the next step. How about helping students take responsibility for both getting their work in on time and for the quality of that work?" She pulled from her own file a chart indicating an individual student's consistency in submitting homework and in providing complete work with each submission.

Several weeks later, Miss Walker asked Mrs. Cummings to come to her classroom. Students were attending to their folders, adding not only individual work, but also check sheets to record their accomplishments, line charts to show their progress, and Pareto diagrams indicating which long division errors were most frequent in their weekly math check-ups.

"I finally figured it out," Miss Walker exclaimed. "Students can use these folders to keep a running record of their own learning. Their data about results or problems has been compiled on visual aids, so they can quickly review their progress by looking at a chart or diagram. They're all very proud of their work."

"And what about parent-teacher-student conferences?" Mrs. Cummings asked.

"Well, data folders have made my life a lot easier," Miss Walker said. "When I met with Victor's parents again, I asked him to show his parents the check sheet he had made to record when his work was submitted. When Victor's own data indicated late submissions and failure to hand things in at all, his parents immediately asked what they could do to help Victor get things in on time."

A = Completed all homework assigned
H = Completed at least half of the assigned homework
L = Completed less than half of the assigned homework
N = Has not completed any of the assigned homework
NH = No homework

Math	A	A	A	A	NH
Reading	L	L	H	H	H
Science	A	NH	NH	A	A
Social Studies	NH	NH	H	NH	NH
	Monday	Tuesday	Wednesday	Thursday	Friday

FIGURE 11.1 Check sheet: My homework data

"It worked like a charm," Miss Walker continued. "The data points were all there. Victor was responsible for it, and they saw the outcome without having to rely only on my assessments. What a breakthrough!"

EXPANDING THE CONCEPT

It is clear that data folders support classroom learning. Part of that learning includes each student's participation in decisions about what goes into the folder. He or she can select samples of best work or choose both a beginning attempt and an accomplished product in order to demonstrate improvement. Charts indicating scores on tests can be part of the data folder, and as teachers and students become increasingly comfortable with the tool, they can add other data tools that reflect the student's learning. Reviewing the tools included in this book will generate ideas for ways to assess and record progress. Some examples of items that may go into a data folder include:

- An affinity diagram reflecting a process of determining a topic for a paper, or an idea for a project.
- Fishbone diagrams to show the relationship between a specific approach and the outcome (for example, reasons for poor performance on a weekly assessment, or factors that contribute to a successful project).
- Check sheets to record homework, behaviors, classroom tasks, and so on.
- Flowcharts for reminding students about how to go about a process, such as long division or checking books out of a library. For younger students, these may include a process for getting ready for dismissal or one for going to the drinking fountain.
- Pareto diagrams that disaggregate data related to specific challenge areas, such as diphthong use in correct spelling, specific math errors, and so on.
- Line graphs to show trends in progress, both up and down, over a period of days, weeks, or months. They may also be used in instructional tasks, such as recording the gerbil's weight each week or recording data from a classroom weather station.
- Lotus diagrams that record personal information. The center square might be labeled "Me," with categories for hobbies, pet peeves, family names, pets, and so on.

In addition to tools for learning and recording progress, data folders can help to tie the daily classroom tasks to long-term goals or expectations. Parents can participate by filling out a form on which they share their own observations about the child.

This form will help me to get to know your child. Please complete and return it to me by September 10. Thank you for participating in your child's education.

Child's name: _____ Nickname: _____

Name(s) of parents or guardians: _____

Phone number: _____ email (optional): _____

Child's birthday: _____ Age: _____

My child is good at: _____
_____

My child needs special help with: _____

My child enjoys: _____

I would like to see my child improve *academically* in the following ways:
_____
_____

I would like to see my child improve *socially* in the following ways:
_____
_____

If there is anything you would like to share about your child that would help to make the school year more successful for him or her, please comment below.
_____
_____

Signature: _____ Date: _____

FIGURE 11.2 Student information form for parents/guardians

Thinking even bigger, students can create individual mission statements related to their hopes and dreams for the year. From those, students can contribute to a classroom mission statement, to be placed in each child's data folder as a reminder of the classroom community's mission. An example of a third-grade mission statement:

"Our third grade mission is to read, write, do math, always do our best, and have fun."

In addition to the classroom mission statement, individual students can create a personal mission statement. While this is not necessary for learning and may seem somewhat artificial to some students, others respond to having such a statement in their data folders.

Beyond the mission statements and specific tools that support learning, data folders may include:

- A statement of goals, both for the classroom and for the individual student. Example: "We will know all our multiplication facts before winter vacation."
- Statements of more specific individual goals within disciplines. Examples: "My goal in math is to have at least four correct answers out of five on my math assessments, and nine correct answers out of ten on open-ended questions, by March 1." Or, "My goal in spelling is to get 80 percent or higher on all spelling tests."
- Behavior goals can be articulated in a data folder as well. These can be recorded on a "behavior calendar" that lists class ground rules and includes space in which students may enter responses to these rules each day.
- Short-cycle assessments—those that assess learning on a frequent, limited basis—should be included in the data folder. A weekly 10-word spelling test, a quick review of multiplication facts, or a review of state capitals might be included in short-cycle assessments to reinforce learning.

WHERE TO BEGIN

Once you have decided that data folders will be useful to support classroom learning, begin to assess what you want to see in those folders, where they will be kept, and when and how data will be entered and charted. The "folder" might not be a folder in the traditional sense, but instead a file box or other container. Your own creativity and that of your students will help to determine content. Each data folder, for example, may include photos of the student at the beginning of the year and later in the year. The student's family might be represented in a photo as well. Remember that the primary purpose of the data folder is to become a learning assessment tool. How much have I learned?

What are my challenges? What else must I learn? These are among the appropriate questions answered by the data folder.

After this plan has been devised, the next step is to develop assessments, check sheets, and charts that will record and display information about what each student is accomplishing. Establishing frequency of assessment, whether weekly, monthly, or other, is important in order to provide students with comparative data on a regular periodic basis.

Defining goals is part of the set-up process for data folders. Determine which tools you might use to help students develop goals both for themselves individually and for the class as a whole.

Bring your students along in the process. They will be eager to set goals, decide which tools to use to record progress, and determine which samples of their own work will go into the data folder.

THE BIG PICTURE: ESTABLISHING DATA CENTERS

The concept of data folders can be applied in a larger way, not only to the classroom but to the entire school or district as well. In this case, data related to mission, goals, milestones, and so on can be kept in one place, available for access by members of the entire school community.

For a classroom data center, larger versions of the tools found in individual data folder can be used. A line chart showing class averages on tests or short-cycle assessments, for example, highlights the progress of the class rather than of the individual. This chart can be displayed prominently along with other tools that assess classroom performance, and the class's mission statement and goals may appear with the display. Both students and parents can access this center for an overview of class goals and dreams, progress in discipline areas, and behavior patterns.

Classroom data centers not only give useful information to the class about its progress, but may also serve as motivators for improvement and for cooperation. For example, to improve a class average, students may find themselves helping those whose poor scores may bring that average down. And knowing that the outcome of an assessment will contribute to a class average will make each student want to do his or her best work.

An even larger application of the data folder concept is represented by a data center for an entire school or district. Just as in the classroom data center, the school's data center will display mission statement, goals for the year, assessment and problem-solving tools that reflect school progress toward improvement and illustrate that progress in visual form, photos of outstanding achievements, and so on. This can be displayed prominently in the school building or, in the case of a district data center, in all buildings.

TEACHERS, TOO...

Teachers are always eager to adapt new approaches to student learning in their classrooms, and data folders offer an opportunity to support that learning. But data folders also provide support for an individual teacher's own learning and professional development, providing a basis for continuous improvement and help in achieving goals.

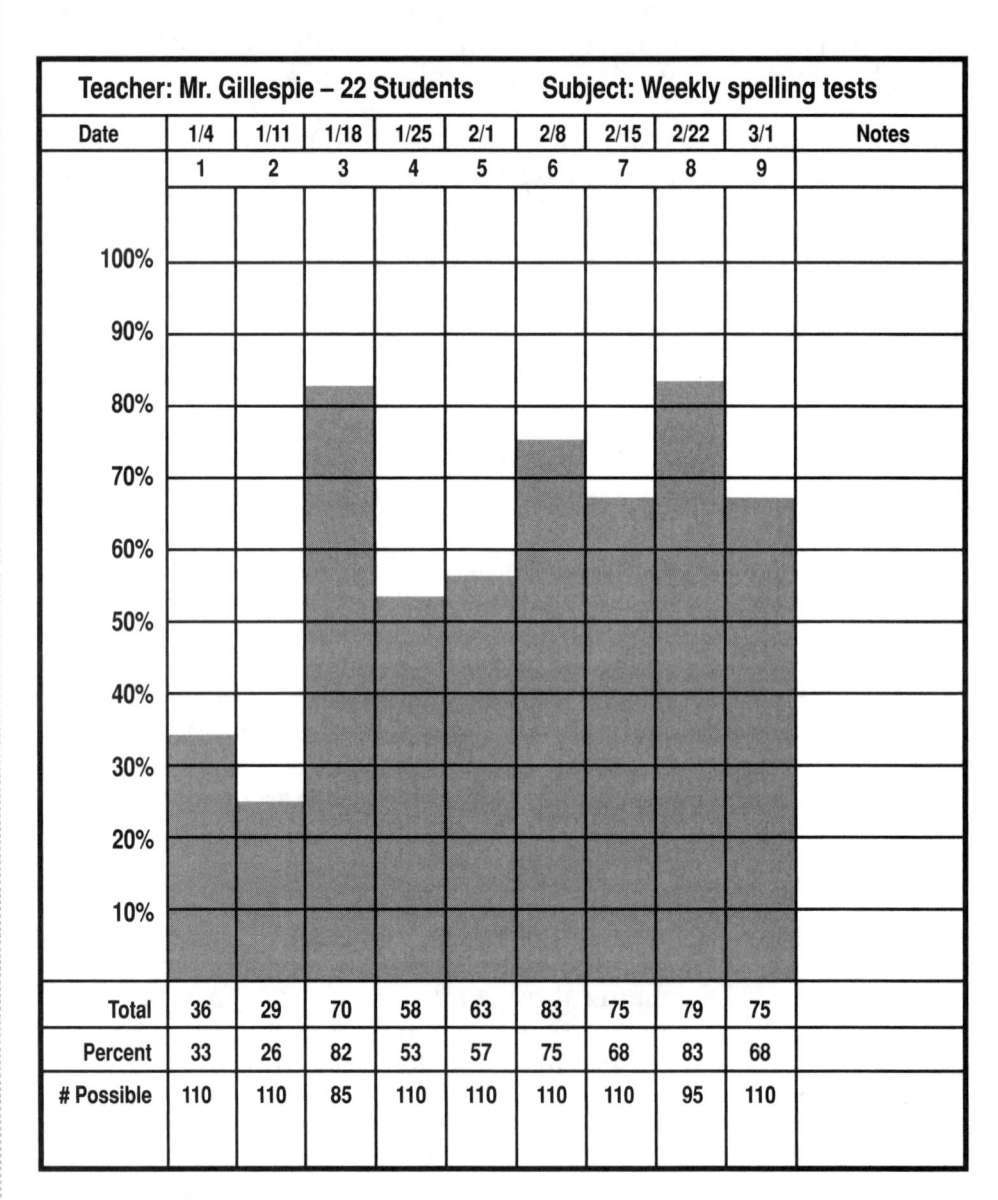

Teacher: Mr. Gillespie – 22 Students						Subject: Weekly spelling tests				
Date	1/4	1/11	1/18	1/25	2/1	2/8	2/15	2/22	3/1	Notes
	1	2	3	4	5	6	7	8	9	
Total	36	29	70	58	63	83	75	79	75	
Percent	33	26	82	53	57	75	68	83	68	
# Possible	110	110	85	110	110	110	110	95	110	

FIGURE 11.3 Class bar graph

To build your own professional data folder, you begin—just as you have with your students—with goals. Your own professional goals, after all, contribute to the goals of the school and the mission of the educational process in your district. As you formulate your own goals, remember that these must be expressed in ways that can be measured. Rather than aspiring to "Increase professional development," for example, consider specific, measurable goals.

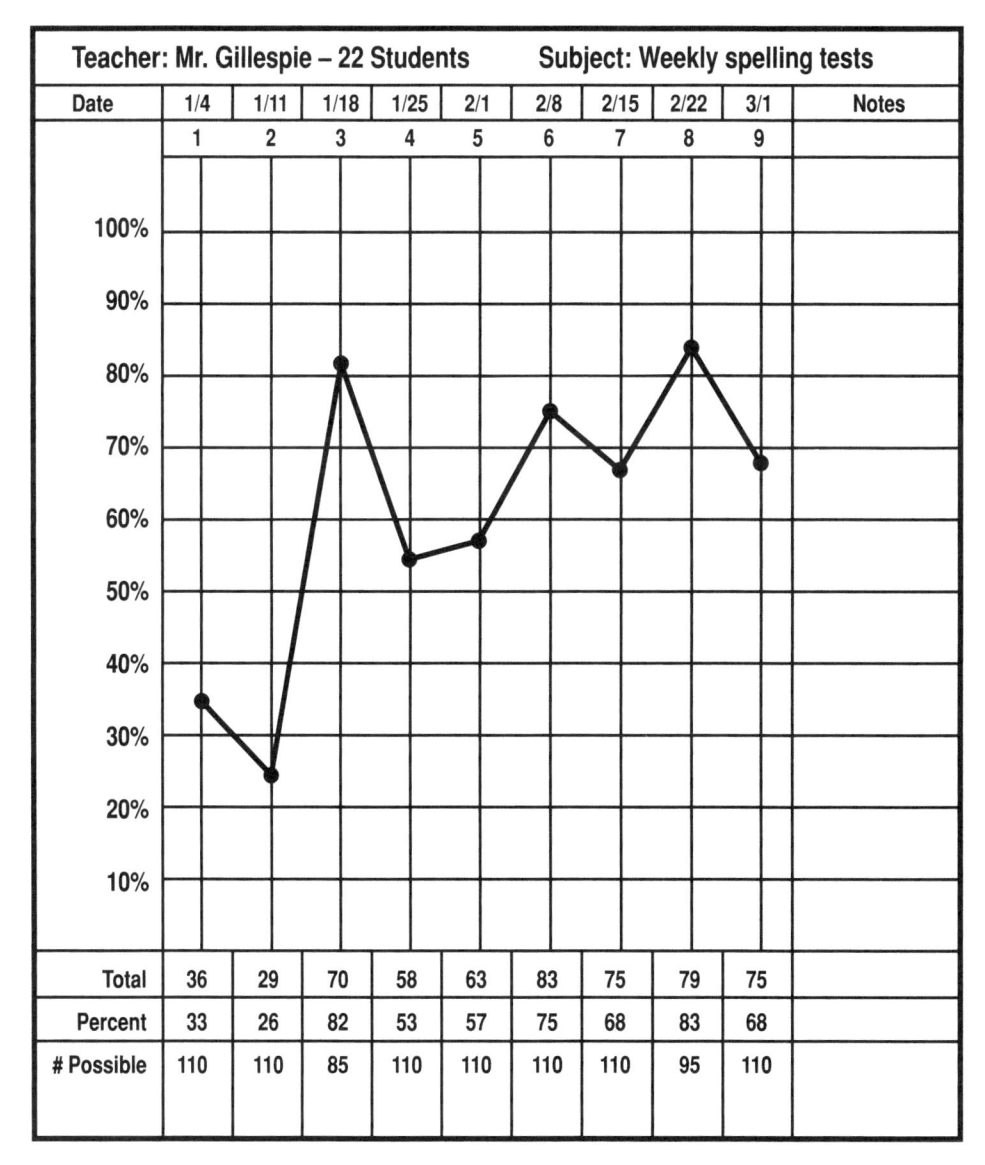

Teacher: Mr. Gillespie – 22 Students					Subject: Weekly spelling tests					
Date	1/4	1/11	1/18	1/25	2/1	2/8	2/15	2/22	3/1	Notes
	1	2	3	4	5	6	7	8	9	
Total	36	29	70	58	63	83	75	79	75	
Percent	33	26	82	53	57	75	68	83	68	
# Possible	110	110	85	110	110	110	110	95	110	

FIGURE 11.4 Class line graph

Among examples of goals that teachers may realistically entertain (and put on a list for their data folders) are the following:

- I will prepare and submit a presentation for a professional conference during this year.
- I will subscribe to a professional journal (name it); after reading it, I will pass it on to a colleague.
- I will learn at least one new strategy for writing an equation from an input-output table.
- I will use quality tools in the classroom at least once each day/week.
- I will post class results for tests and other assessments on a regular basis, using check sheets and line charts.
- I will develop rubrics for all assignments, involving students as appropriate in developing these rubrics.
- I will support my own good health by exercising at least three times each week.
- I will improve my fluency with Spanish by listening to language tapes during my commute to school.
- I will initiate a recycling program in my classroom by engaging students in a discussion about the value of re-using paper and recycling materials as appropriate.

Notice that these are not "resolutions," or wish lists, but specific goals that will require action in order to be executed fully. At the end of the year (or other appropriate period of time), the list itself can provide material for a discussion with colleagues and supervising principals. More importantly, it offers food for reflection about one's own professional development and growth within the profession.

SUGGESTIONS FOR USING DATA FOLDERS:

- Gather data using appropriate tools described in earlier chapters.
- Enlist the help of students in determining which tools are to be used to reflect each task.
- Emphasize the visual aspects of the tools that will go into the data folder.
- Be sure that enough data has been collected to render the tools useful, as well as to demonstrate trends that can be seen in the data folder.
- Be open to including materials that are suggested by students. Primary criterion for determining what goes into a data folder should be how well each item reflects the student's learning.

- Remember that all disciplines should be represented in the data folder—not just reading and math—in order to provide a complete picture of progress in learning.
- Invite students to review their data folders frequently, and to identify trends that they may see.
- Make data folders available to parents during formal and informal conferences.
- Encourage the students to lead parent-teacher-student conferences, using the data folder as a primary communication tool.

NOW IT'S YOUR TURN...

Using the tools described in earlier chapters, keep track of student progress in classroom learning as well as behavioral goals. Keep these in your data folder and review them frequently in order to identify trends.

Examples of items that may be included in data folders, your own or those of your students:

- Individual goals for the year
- A copy of goals that the class has agreed on
- A check sheet indicating completion of homework assignments
- A cause-and-effect diagram detailing factors that have contributed to a successful project or report
- A list of books read or poems shared
- A line chart showing test scores or short-cycle assessment results
- A Pareto diagram indicating sources of problems in math computations
- A flow chart that tracks progress toward a specific goal
- Examples of student handwriting from early in the school year
- A descriptive writing exercise, with concrete language circled
- A chart of the number of concrete verbs or nouns used in a descriptive paper
- A check sheet with weekly tardies or absences
- An affinity diagram that helps categorize a topic being studied
- A lotus diagram reflecting the process followed in order to find a topic for a writing exercise

Use your imagination! Think of ways to show how well you are learning and meeting goals, and use tools that show where your greatest learning challenges lie. Your own creativity will make the data folder really yours, and something that will give a complete picture of the kinds of progress you are making. This is true both for your students and for yourself. In either case, the data folder provides a point of departure for discussion (with parents, principal, group leader), an opportunity for reflection, and a sense of progress toward goals throughout the year.

Examples of tools related to math progress that might be a part of student portfolios:

I will get at least _____ right out of 30 on my math facts.

Name:_____

30					
29					
28					
27					
26					
25					
24					
23					
22					
21					
20					
19					
18					
17					
16					
15					
14					
13					
12					
11					
10					
9					
8					
7					
6					
5					
4					
3					
2					
1					
Day	Monday	Tuesday	Wednesday	Thursday	Friday
Date	10/2	10/3	10/4	10/5	10/6

FIGURE 11.5 "Mad Minute" math facts assessment results

Name:	Sam				Subject:	Math				
Date	1/4	1/11	1/18	1/25	2/1	2/8	2/15	2/22	3/1	Notes
	1	2	3	4	5	6	7	8	9	
Total	2	2	4	3	3	3	3	4	5	
Percent										
# Possible	5	5	5	5	5	5	5	5	5	
Standard 1	1	1	1	1	1	1	1	1	1	
Standard 2	0	0	0	0	1	1	1	1	1	
Standard 3	0	1	1	1	0	0	0	0	1	
Standard 4	1	0	1	1	0	1	1	1	1	
Standard 5	0	0	1	1	1	1	0	1	1	

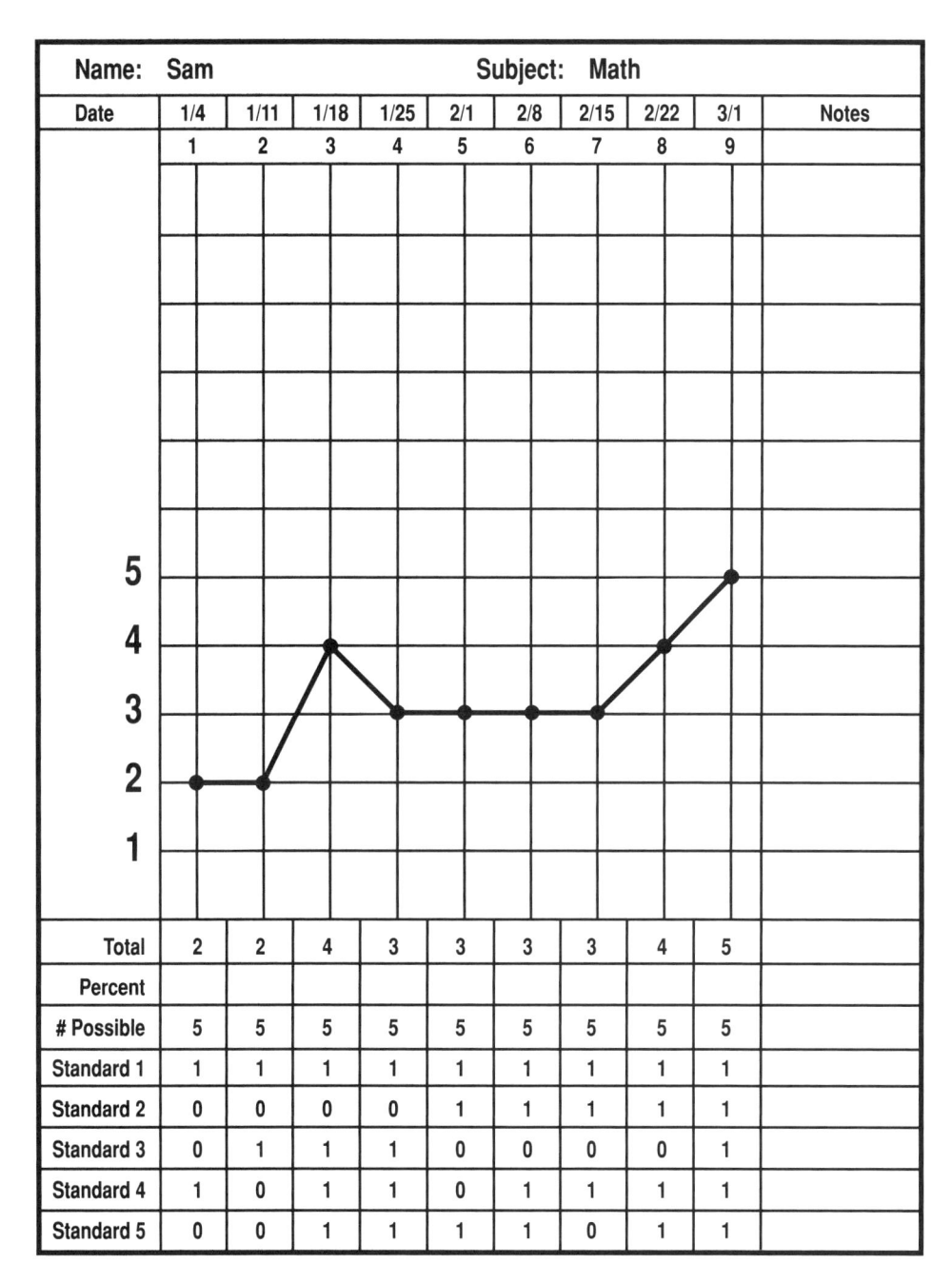

FIGURE 11.6 Math line graph

Name:	Sam					Subject:	Math			
Date	1/4	1/11	1/18	1/25	2/1	2/8	2/15	2/22	3/1	Notes
	1	2	3	4	5	6	7	8	9	
Total	2	2	4	3	3	3	3	4	5	
Percent										
# Possible	5	5	5	5	5	5	5	5	2	
Standard 1	1	1	1	1	1	1	1	1	1	
Standard 2	0	0	0	0	1	1	1	1	1	
Standard 3	0	1	1	1	0	0	0	0	1	
Standard 4	1	0	1	0	0	0	1	1	1	
Standard 5	0	0	1	1	1	1	0	1	1	

FIGURE 11.7 Math bar graph

It's easy to see how visual records such as these can be created from any measurable data. Whether you and your students want to record the number of chapter books read or to create a flow chart for a process to assure completion of homework assignments, there are tools available to support those efforts.

An art teacher uses check sheets with students to help them review their use of specific art genres (watercolor, charcoal, and so on) or assignments. You can use similar tools in your classroom. The portfolio is always open—add your own contents!

SUGGESTIONS FOR FURTHER READING

FOR READING ABOUT TOOLS:

Buzan, Tony, and Barry Buzan. 1994. *The mind map book: How to use radiant thinking to maximize your brain's untapped potential.* New York: Dutton.

Cleary, Barbara A., and Sally J. Duncan. 1997. *Tools and techniques to inspire classroom learning.* Milwaukee: ASQ Quality Press.

Cleary, Michael J. et al. 1995. *Total quality tools for education (K–12).* Dayton: PQ Systems, Inc.

———. 1996. *Pocket tools for education.* Dayton: PQ Systems, Inc.

FOR READING ABOUT THE IMPROVEMENT CYCLE:

Ball, M. et al. *Total quality transformation* 1994. Dayton, OH: PQ Systems, Inc.

Deming, W. Edwards. 1986. *Out of the crisis.* Cambridge, Mass.: MIT Center for Advanced Engineering Study.

Langford, David P., and Barbara A. Cleary. 1995. *Orchestrating learning with quality.* Milwaukee: ASQ Quality Press.

FOR READING ABOUT LEARNING AND THINKING:

Abbott, John. 1997. To be intelligent. *Educational Leadership,* March.

Armstrong, T. 1993. *Seven kinds of smart: Identifying and developing your many intelligences.* New York: Plume.

Brandt, Ron. 1997. On using knowledge about our brain: A conversation with Bob Sylwester. *Educational Leadership* 54: 6 (March).

Caine, R. N., and G. Caine. 1991. *Making connections: Teaching and the human brain.* Alexandria VA: ASCD.

———. 1990. Understanding a brain-based approach to learning and teaching. *Educational Leadership* 48, 2: 66–70.

Gardner, Howard. 1983. *Frames of mind: The theory of multiple intelligences.* New York: Basic Books.

———. 1991. *The unschooled mind: How children think and how schools should teach.* New York: Basic Books.

Hart, L. 1975. *How the brain works: A new understanding of human learning, emotion, and thinking.* New York: Basic Books.

Healy, Jane. 1987. *Your child's growing mind: A guide to learning and brain development from birth to adolescence.* Garden City, NY: Doubleday.

———. 1990. *Endangered minds: Why children don't think and what we can do about it.* New York: Touchstone Books, Simon & Schuster.

Markova, D. 1992. *How your child is smart: A life-changing approach to learning.* Berkeley, CA: Conari Press.

Nummela, R., and T. Rosengran. 1986. What's happening in students' brains may redefine teaching. *Educational Leadership* 43, 8: 49–53.

Sternberg, R. J. 1995. *In search of the human mind.* Orlando, FL: Harcourt Brace College Publishers.

———. 1997. What does it mean to be smart? *Educational Leadership* 54: 6 (March).

Sternberg, R. J., and L. Spear-Swerling. 1996. *Teaching for thinking.* Washington, D.C.: American Psychological Association.

Sylwester, Robert. 1995. *A celebration of neurons: An educator's guide to the human brain.* Alexandria, VA: ASCD.

GLOSSARY

Affinity Relationship or similarity; items that fall into the same category or classification have an *affinity* to each other. See chapter 2, "Affinity Exercises."

Average A number found by adding numbers of subgroups together and dividing by the total number of subgroups. A statisticalm concept important to understanding variation.

Bar chart Visual display of data by charting it according to subgroup size in order to garner further information about the data. See *Pareto* and *histogram*.

Brainstorming By using specific guidelines, generating ideas in a free-flowing way from all members of a group. See chapter 1, "Brainstorming." Compare *Crawford slip process*.

Cause-and-effect chart Also known *fishbone diagram* because of its resemblance to the spine and bones of a fish skeleton. Used to record possible causes for a problem or for a success, and to classify these according to predetermined labels. See chapter 4, "Fishbone Diagrams."

Check sheet A tool that organizes the collection of data (see chapter 6, "Check Sheets"). Its format is flexible to provide for a variety of kinds of data. Often organized in columns and rows, with data occurrences, checked off, but other information may be written on a checksheet as well.

Continuous improvement A process of studying a problem or situation, gathering data that relates to it, developing a theory for improving it, testing the theory on a small scale, reevaluating data in light of the improvement theory, putting it into practice, and looking for additional ways to improve the problem or situation. See *PDSA cycle*.

Crawford slip process A kind of brainstorming using small slips of paper to record ideas. Often used in affinity exercises, or for situations that are complex or controversial. See chapter 1, "Brainstorming."

Facilitator One who provides a bridge to learning or creates an environment for learning by monitoring a process. A teacher is a kind of facilitator, but students may serve this role as well.

176 GLOSSARY

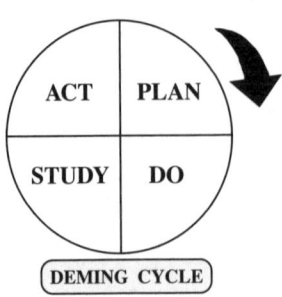

Fishbone diagram A tool that helps discern contributing factors to an outcome or problem. Also known as a cause-and-effect chart. Causes are recorded on the *bones* of the fish—hence its name. See chapter 4, Fishbone Diagrams."

Flowchart A visual documentation of a process. A flowchart illustrates the step-by-step approach to a specific process by using a series of symbols to denote tasks, decision points, and stages in the flow of the process. See chapter 7, "Flowcharts."

Histogram A bar chart that provides a visual representation of data. Bars are arranged in order with respect to time, size, volume, and so on. Similar to Pareto diagrams (see chapter 10) except with respect to the order of the data. See chapter 8, "Histograms."

Line graph Also known as *run chart*. Promotes analysis of data by illustrating patterns or trends over a period of time. Data points are entered in time order and connected. See chapter 9, "Line Graphs."

Nominal group technique A method of determining consensus by allowing all team members to designate items with their greatest support. This problem-solving tool narrows a list of brainstormed items down until the best ideas are selected.

Nonnormal A distribution of data that does not reflect the bell curve, but is skewed in some way, showing uneven distribution. Like normal distribution, this statistical concept provides a way to understand data after it has been collected.

Normal curve, normal distribution Patterns that can be seen in data by means of a histogram (see chapter 8, "Histograms"). This arrangement of data is bell-shaped, with tapering ends that indicate fewer data points on either side of a central curve. Also known as a *bell curve*.

Pareto diagram A bar chart that gives a visual representation of data, in order of its frequency. The first bar reflects the greatest number of occurrences, with others in descending order to the smallest group. Named after Italian economist Vilfredo Pareto. See chapter 10, "Pareto Diagrams."

PDSA cycle Plan-do-study-act, a cycle that reflects the continuous improvement process, represents the scientific method as applied to improvement and problem solving. Sometimes called the Shewhart cycle, for statistician Walter Shewhart, or the Deming cycle, widely practiced by organizational philosopher W. Edwards Deming.

Process Individual processes make up systems. A process, like a system, involves a series of steps that are undertaken in order to get to completion. Most processes can be recorded by means of flowcharts (see chapter 5).

Root cause Also known as *main cause*. An underlying contributor to an outcome or problem that seems to have the greatest influence. Both fishbone diagrams (see chapter 4) and relations diagrams (see chapter 5) are tools that help identify root causes.

Run chart See *line graph*. Name derives from the arrangement of data in a *run,* or in the order of its occurrence.

Scaling Numbers that are written on the left bar of a chart so that data can be plotted. Different kinds of diagrams and charts have different kinds of scaling.

Scaling, histograms:

(a) For vertical axis: From your check sheet, observe the frequency of each class. (How many occurrences does it have?) Number the vertical axis so that every frequency will fit on the chart. For example, if there are 10 occurrences for one of your classes, be sure to number the axis so it goes at least to 10. To decide increments, or what numbers to put on the axis: Find the number in the largest group, and subtract the number in the smallest group from that. Then divide by the number of groups (classes) you have. This should indicate the increments between the numbers. For example, for the height histogram in chapter 8, the greatest number is 18, and the smallest is 16. Subtract 2 from 18 (16), then divide by the number of groups, 7. You will have 2.2. Create a chart with increments of 2 or 3.

(b) For horizontal axis: This is where the classes (groups) go. You will divide your continuous line to make groups of volume, time, distance, and so on. To determine the number of classes, use this rough guideline:

No. of data points	No. of classes
Under 50	5–8
50–100	6–10
100–250	7–12
Over 250	10–20

Next, find the width of the class, using the same formula as in part a above. Subtract the smallest value in the data from the largest value, then divide by the number of classes (from guideline above). For Ariyah's penny collections in chapter 8, the largest value is 51.63, and the smallest is 12.50. He subtracted, then divided by the number of classes or groups.

Scaling, Pareto charts:

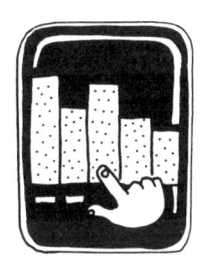

(a) For horizontal axis: Divide this into the same number of equal parts as there are categories. Chris, in chapter 9, had 10 different categories of birds (Figure 10.2). If there are several categories with very small numbers, it is acceptable to include a category entitled "other" or "miscellaneous," but it is preferable to avoid this.

(b) For vertical axis: Label this with the units of measurement such as frequency, hours, and so on. To be accurate, the vertical axis should include enough space for a cumulative total of all of the categories. Since this would create a very tall chart in some cases, the vertical axis is constructed to accommodate the largest category rather than the cumulative amounts. This depends on your purpose. The charts in chapter 10 do not accommodate the cumulative numbers and percentages. If you would like more information about creating Pareto diagrams, see "Suggestions for Further Reading."

Scaling, line graphs

(a) For horizontal axis: Use the number of points in the data set. (For example, if there are 30 days, use 30 points across the bottom of the graph.)

(b) For vertical axis: Use a rule similar to that for histograms, above. That is, subtract the smallest from the largest. Then divide by a number that represents two-thirds of the points along the horizontal axis. This will suggest the incremental value for scaling the line graph on the left, vertical axis.

System A collection of processes and people that are aligned toward serving a common purpose or aim (Cleary & Duncan, 1997). A system includes the factors or materials that provide input, output, support, and feedback.

Thinking tool A method or approach that supports thinking and learning. Contributes to the process of learning rather than being an end in itself. Tools in this book support thinking in this way, and there are many other thinking tools as well.

Variation A characteristic of a process. Natural variation can be observed on a line graph (see chapter 9). Further statistical analysis of variation is possible by means of control charts and other tools. Line graphs form the basis for control charts, which show how stable and predictable a process really is.

INDEX

A

Affinity diagrams and data folders, 162
Affinity exercises and brainstorming, 6, 11, 25, 27
   and check sheets, 25
   Crawford slip method, 22, 25
   for Fourth of July, 22–23
   "Home Connection," 30
   and lotus flower diagrams, 25, 40
   "My Own Thinking Tools Page," 27–30
   and Pareto diagrams, 25
   and relations diagrams, 25
   suggestions for using, 24
   tools to use with, 24–25
   topics for, 29–30
Assessment, frequency of, 165

B

Bar charts. See Histograms
Bar graphs and data folders, 166, 172
Bell curves, 119
Brainstorming, 2–17
   and affinity exercises, 6, 11, 25, 27
   Crawford slip method, 10, 22, 25
   definition of, 4–5
   facilitators for, 13
   and fishbone diagrams, 11, 50, 51, 53
   and flowcharts, 11, 97
   and histograms, 11
   and hitchhiking, 5
   "Home Connection," 15
   judgment about ideas, 6, 28, 53
   list for science fair projects, 5–6, 9
   and lotus flower diagrams, 11, 35, 40
   "My Own Thinking Tools Page," 13–14
   narrowing the list, 6–9
   and Pareto diagrams, 11
   and piggy-backing, 5
   purpose of, 5
   and relations diagrams, 66, 69, 73
   suggestions for use, 10
   tools to use with, 11
   topics for, 13, 15
   uses for, 8
   See also Nominal group technique

C

Cause-and-effect relationships, 49
   relations diagrams, 65
   See also Fishbone diagrams
Check sheets, 78–87
   and affinity exercises, 25
   columns (down) and rows (across), 80, 81
   data collection, 81
   and data folders, 162
   and fishbone diagrams, 53
   and flowcharts, 82, 95, 96, 97
   forms of, 80
   and histograms, 82, 111, 112, 113, 115
   "Home Connection," 85–86
   and line graphs, 82, 131, 132
   and lotus flower diagrams, 40
   "My homework data," 161
   "My Own Thinking Tools Page," 83–85
   and Pareto diagrams, 82, 143, 144, 147
   and relations diagrams, 69
   for science fair projects, 4
   suggestions for use, 81
   tools to use with, 82
   topics, 85, 86
Classification of data, Pareto diagram, 153
Classroom data centers, 165
Columns (down) and rows (across), check sheets, 80, 81
Complex issues, and relations diagrams, 68
Consensus, 7, 8

Continuums versus categories
　histograms, 113
　Pareto diagrams, 152
Crawford slip method
　for affinity exercises, 22, 25
　for brainstorming, 10, 25

D

Daily work portfolio. *See* Data folders
Data centers, 165
Data collection
　check sheets, 81
　histograms, 114, 120
　line graphs, 127
Data folders, 158–172
　and parental support, 160, 161, 163, 169
　and student involvement, 168–169
　suggested contents for, 160, 162, 164–165, 169–170
　suggestions for using, 168–169
　used by teachers, 166–168
Data points, histograms, 114
Decision points, flowcharts, 93, 94, 95
Distributions, histograms, 119

F

Facilitators for brainstorming, 13
Family tree diagram, relations diagrams, 65
Fishbone diagrams, 48–59
　and brainstorming, 11, 50, 51, 53
　cause-and-effect diagrams, 49, 66
　and check sheets, 53
　and data folders, 162
　and flowcharts, 49, 92, 96, 97
　and histograms, 115
　"Home Connection," 58
　and line graphs, 53, 130, 132
　and lotus flower diagrams, 40
　and main causes, 49, 50, 51
　"My Own Thinking Tools Page," 55–58
　and Pareto diagrams, 147
　in planning, 53
　for processes, 48, 50
　purpose of, 49
　and relations diagrams, 66
　step-by-step approach, 53
　suggestions for using, 53
　tools to use with, 53
　topics, 56, 57, 58

Flowcharts, 90–105
　and brainstorming, 11, 97
　and check sheets, 82, 95, 96, 97
　and data folders, 162
　decision points, 93, 94, 95
　and fishbone diagrams, 92, 96, 97
　"Home Connection," 104
　and line graphs, 97
　"My Own Thinking Tools Page," 99–104
　problem-solving, 91
　process, 92
　and relations diagrams, 69
　symbols for, 92, 93, 105
　tools to use with, 97
　topics, 103–104
Fourth of July affinity exercise, 22–23

G

Grouping tools, 21
　See also Affinity exercises
Groups, 5
　consensus in, 7, 8
　and relations diagrams, 72
　See also Teams

H

Histograms, 108–123
　and bar charts, 112
　bell curves, 119
　and brainstorming, 11
　and check sheets, 82, 111, 112, 113, 115
　continuums versus categories, 113
　data collection, 114
　data points, 114
　distributions, 119
　and fishbone diagrams, 115
　"Home Connection," 120–121
　and line graphs, 111, 115, 127, 131
　"My Own Thinking Tools Page," 117–120
　normal curves, 119
　and Pareto diagrams, 111, 113, 152
　scale for, 112, 114
　sorting, 110
　suggestions for using, 114
　tools to use with, 115
　topics, 120–121
Hitchhiking and brainstorming, 5

"Home Connection"
  affinity exercises, 30
  brainstorming, 15
  check sheets, 85–86
  fishbone diagrams, 58
  flowcharts, 104
  histograms, 120–121
  line graphs, 137
  lotus flower diagrams, 42–43
  Pareto diagrams, 153
  relations diagrams, 73

I

Individuals versus teams, 4
Issues, challenges, or problems. *See* Topics

J

Judgment about ideas, brainstorming, 6, 28, 53

L

Line graphs, 126–139, 151
  and check sheets, 82, 131, 132
  data collection, 127
  and data folders, 162, 166, 171
  and fishbone diagrams, 53, 130, 132
  and histograms, 111, 115, 127, 131
  "Home Connection," 137
  and lotus flower diagrams, 132
  "My Own Thinking Tools
    Page," 133–136
  and Pareto diagrams, 127, 130, 132, 147
  and pie charts, 127
  run charts, 127
  scale for, 134
  suggestions for using, 131–132
  time order, 132
  tools to use with, 132
  topics, 134, 135, 137
  trends and patterns, 132
Lotus flower diagrams, 34–45
  and affinity exercises, 25, 40
  blank diagram, 36
  and brainstorming, 11, 35, 40
  and check sheets, 40
  and data folders, 162

  and fishbone diagrams, 40
  "Home Connection," 42–43
  and line graphs, 132
  "My Own Thinking Tools
    Page," 41–42
  process of, 35–38
  suggestions for using, 39
  tools to use with, 40
  topics for, 35, 39, 41, 43

M

"Mad Minute" math facts assessment results, 170
Main causes and fishbone diagrams,
    49, 50, 51
"My Own Thinking Tools Page"
  affinity exercises, 27–30
  brainstorming, 13–14
  check sheets, 83–85
  fishbone diagrams, 55–58
  flowcharts, 99–104
  histograms, 117–120
  line graphs, 133–136
  lotus flower diagrams, 41–42
  Pareto diagrams, 149–152
  relations diagrams, 71–73
Mission statements, 164

N

Nominal group technique
  for brainstorming lists, 6–9
  preliminary ranking, 7–9
  rules for, 6–7
Normal curves, histograms, 119

P

Pareto diagrams, 142–155
  and affinity exercises, 25
  and brainstorming, 11
  and check sheets, 82, 143, 144, 147
  classification of data, 153
  continuums versus categories, 152
  and data folders, 162
  and fishbone diagrams, 147
  and histograms, 111, 113, 152
  "Home Connection," 153

181

and line graphs, 127, 130, 132, 147
"My Own Thinking Tools Page," 149–152
and relations diagrams, 69
scale for, 144
suggestions for using, 147
tools to use with, 147
topics, 151, 152, 153
Patterns and trends, line graphs, 132
Pie charts, 127
Piggy-backing and brainstorming, 5
Planning and fishbone diagrams, 53
Preliminary ranking, nominal group technique, 7–9
Problem solving, 8, 91

R

Relations diagrams, 62–75, 113
   and affinity exercises, 25
   arrows out and in, 67
   and brainstorming, 66, 69, 73
   cause-and-effect relationships, 65, 66
   and check sheets, 69
   and complex issues, 68
   definition, 68
   family tree diagram, 65
   and flowcharts, 69
   and groups, 72
   "Home Connection," 73
   "My Own Thinking Tools Page," 71–73
   and Pareto diagrams, 69
   process, 65–66
   suggestions for using, 68–69
   and teams, 66
   tools to use with, 69
   topics, 71, 72, 73
Root causes. *See* Main causes
Rules for nominal group technique, 6–7
Run charts. *See* Line graphs

S

Scale
   for histograms, 112, 114
   for line graphs, 134
   for Pareto diagrams, 144
School district data centers, 165
Science fair projects, 2–9
Sorting, 21–22
   See also Affinity exercises
Student information form for parents/guardians, 163
Symbols for flowcharts, 92, 93, 105

T

Teachers, data folders for professional development of, 166–168
Teams
   and nominal group technique, 7
   and relations diagrams, 66
   for science fair projects, 4
   versus individuals, 4
   See also Groups
Themes. *See* Topics
Time order, line graphs, 132
Topics
   affinity exercises, 29–30
   brainstorming, 13, 15
   check sheets, 85, 86
   fishbone diagrams, 56, 57, 58
   flowcharts, 103–104
   histograms, 120–121
   line graphs, 134, 135, 137
   lotus flower diagrams, 35, 39, 41, 43
   Pareto diagrams, 151, 152, 153
   relations diagrams, 71, 72, 73
Trends and patterns
   data folders used to identify, 169–170
   line graphs, 132

V

Visual aids in data folders, 161
Voting, 7